GCSE OCR Gateway
Chemistry
Higher Workbook

This book is for anyone doing **GCSE OCR Gateway Chemistry** at higher level.

It's full of **tricky questions**... each one designed to make you **sweat** — because that's the only way you'll get any **better**.

There are questions to see **what facts** you know. There are questions to see how well you can **apply those facts**. And there are questions to see what you know about **how science works**.

It's also got some daft bits in to try and make the whole experience at least vaguely entertaining for you.

What CGP is all about

Our sole aim here at CGP is to produce the highest quality books — carefully written, immaculately presented and dangerously close to being funny.

Then we work our socks off to get them out to you — at the cheapest possible prices.

Contents

CHEMCIAL CONCEPTS

Chemcial Formulas 1
Chemical Equations 2

MODULE C1 — CARBON CHEMISTRY

Food Additives 3
Food Packaging 5
Cooking and Chemical Change 7
Perfumes 8
Kinetic Theory & Forces Between Particles 9
Solutions 11
Polymers 12
Polymers and Their Uses 13
Alkanes and Alkenes 14
Fractional Distillation of Crude Oil 15
Hydrocarbon Properties — Bonds 17
Cracking 18
Fuels from Crude Oil 20
Burning Fuels 21
Energy Transfer in Reactions 22
Measuring the Energy Content of Fuels 23
Mixed Questions — Module C1 24

MODULE C2 — ROCKS AND METALS

Paints and Pigments 27
Dyes and Special Pigments 28
Construction Materials 29
Extracting Pure Copper 30
Alloys 31
Building Cars 33
The Three Different Types of Rock 34
The Earth's Structure 36
Evidence for Plate Tectonics 38
Volcanic Eruptions 40
The Evolution of the Atmosphere 42
The Carbon Cycle 44
Air Pollution and Acid Rain 45
Chemical Reaction Rates 46
Collision Theory 47
Mixed Questions — Module C2 50

MODULE C3 — THE PERIODIC TABLE

Atoms 53
Isotopes, Elements and Compounds 54
The Periodic Table 55
Electron Shells 56
Ionic Bonding 58
Ions and Ionic Compounds 59
Group 1 — Alkali Metals 60
Electrolysis and the Half-Equations 62
Extracting Aluminium 63
Covalent Bonding 65

Group 7 — Halogens 66
Metals 68
Superconductors and Transition Metals 70
Thermal Decomposition and Precipitation 71
Mixed Questions — Module C3 73

MODULE C4 — CHEMICAL ECONOMICS

Acids and Bases 76
Reactions of Acids 78
Relative Formula Mass 80
Calculating Masses in Reactions 81
Percentage Yield 83
Fertilisers 84
The Haber Process 86
Minimising the Cost of Production 87
Detergents and Dry-Cleaning 88
Chemical Production 91
Allotropes of Carbon 93
Water Purity 95
Mixed Questions — Module C4 97

MODULE C5 — HOW MUCH?

The Mole 100
Reacting Masses and Empirical Formulas 101
Electrolysis 102
Electrolysis — Calculating Masses 105
Concentration 107
Titrations 110
More on Titration 111
Gas Volumes 113
Following Reactions 114
Equilibrium 116
Changing Equilibrium 117
The Contact Process 119
Strong and Weak Acids 120
Precipitation Reactions 122
Preparing Insoluble Salts 123
Mixed Questions — Module C5 124

MODULE C6 — CHEMISTRY OUT THERE

Redox and Displacement Reactions 127
Rusting of Iron 129
Fuel Cells 130
Alcohols 132
Salt 134
CFCs and the Ozone Layer 136
Hardness of Water 139
Fats and Oils 141
Using Plant Oils 143
Drugs 144
Aspirin 145
Mixed Questions — Module C6 146

Published by Coordination Group Publications Ltd.

From original material by Paddy Gannon.

Editors:
Ellen Bowness, Sarah Hilton, Sharon Keeley, Kate Redmond, Ami Snelling.

Contributors:
Michael Aicken, Mike Bossart, Mike Dagless, Ian H Davis, John Duffy, Max Fishel,
Rebecca Harvey, Lucy Muncaster, Andy Rankin, Sidney Stringer Community School,
Paul Warren, Chris Workman.

ISBN: 978 1 84146 571 5

With thanks to Barrie Crowther and Glenn Rogers for the proofreading.
With thanks to Jan Nash and Katie Steele for the copyright research.

Data used to construct pie chart on page 77 from "Concise Dictionary of Chemistry"
edited by Daintith, J (1986). By permission of Oxford University Press. www.oup.com

Graph of the Haber Process on page 117 from "Chemistry for AQA" by Ann and Paterick Fullick.
Reprinted by permission of Harcourt Education.

GORE-TEX®, GORE®, and designs are registered trademarks of W L Gore and Associates.
This book contains copyrighted material reproduced with the permission of W.L. Gore and Associates.
Copyright 2006 W.L. Gore and Associates.

Groovy website: www.cgpbooks.co.uk

Printed by Elanders Hindson Ltd, Newcastle upon Tyne.
Jolly bits of clipart from CorelDRAW®

Chemical Formulas

Q1   The **displayed** formula for **ethanol** is shown below.

H–C–C–O–H with H atoms (displayed structure)

a)   In a molecule of ethanol, what is the total number of atoms of:

   i) carbon?   ....

   ii) hydrogen?   ....

b)   What is the molecular formula of ethanol?   ....

Q2   Complete the table on the right showing the **displayed formulas** and **molecular formulas** of three carbon compounds.

DISPLAYED FORMULA	MOLECULAR FORMULA
H–C–H (with H above and below)	a)
H–C–C–H (with H above and below each C)	b)
H–C–C–C–H (with H above and below each C)	c)

Q3   Follow the steps to find the formula of **iron(II) carbonate**.

a)   What is the charge on an iron(II) ion?   ....

b)   What is the charge on a carbonate ion?   ....

c)   What is the formula of iron(II) carbonate?   ....

Q4   Use the table to work out the **formulas** of the following compounds.

Positive Ions						Negative Ions	
Lithium	Li^+	Barium	Ba^{2+}	Zinc	Zn^{2+}	Chloride	Cl^-
Sodium	Na^+	Magnesium	Mg^{2+}	Manganese(II)	Mn^{2+}	Hydroxide	OH^-
Potassium	K^+	Iron(II)	Fe^{2+}	Aluminium	Al^{3+}	Oxide	O^{2-}
		Copper(II)	Cu^{2+}	Iron(III)	Fe^{3+}	Carbonate	CO_3^{2-}

a)   magnesium oxide   ....

b)   potassium chloride   ....

c)   copper(II) carbonate   ....

d)   sodium hydroxide   ....

e)   iron(III) hydroxide   ....

Chemical Equations

Q1 Here is the equation for the production of carbon **mon**oxide from a poorly ventilated charcoal flame. It is **not** balanced correctly.

$$C + O_2 \rightarrow CO$$

Circle the **correctly balanced** version of this equation.

$$C + O_2 \rightarrow CO_2$$

$$C + O_2 \rightarrow 2CO$$

$$2C + O_2 \rightarrow 2CO$$

Q2 A book describes a reaction as follows: "**Methane** (CH_4) burns in **oxygen** (O_2) to form **carbon dioxide** (CO_2) and **water** (H_2O)."

a) What are the **reactants** and the **products** in this reaction?

Reactants: .... Products: ....

b) Write the **word equation** for this reaction.

....

c) Write the **balanced symbol equation** for the reaction.

....

─Don't forget — the oxygen─
─ ends up in both products. ─

Q3 Add **one** number to each of these equations so that they are **correctly balanced**.

a) .... CuO + ... HBr → .... $CuBr_2$ + ... H_2O

b) .... H_2 + ... Br_2 → .... HBr

c) .... Mg + ... O_2 → $2MgO$

d) $2NaOH$ + ... H_2SO_4 → .... Na_2SO_4 + ... H_2O

─ I've left spaces in front of all the ─
─ molecules so I don't give the game ─
─ away. If a molecule doesn't need a ─
─ number in front, just leave it blank. ─

Q4 **Balance** these equations.

a) .... $NaOH$ + ... $AlBr_3$ → .... $NaBr$ + ... $Al(OH)_3$

b) .... $FeCl_2$ + ... Cl_2 → .... $FeCl_3$

c) .... Fe + ... O_2 → .... Fe_2O_3

d) .... NH_3 + ... O_2 → .... NO + ... H_2O

e) .... MgO + ... HNO_3 → .... $Mg(NO_3)_2$ + ... H_2O

f) .... $CuSO_4$ + ... $NaOH$ → .... $Cu(OH)_2$ + ... Na_2SO_4

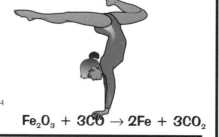

$$Fe_2O_3 + 3CO \rightarrow 2Fe + 3CO_2$$

Top Tip: Balancing equations is a simple matter of **trial and error** — changing one thing at a time until eventually you get the same number of each atom on both sides.

Food Additives

Q1   Draw lines to match up each type of **food additive** with its **function**.

colouring

flavour enhancer

antioxidant

emulsifier

improves the natural taste and smell of food

prevents oils separating and floating on top of water

makes foods look more appealing

makes food stay fresh for longer

Q2   Sue decides to find out about **additives**. She goes to her local supermarket and looks at the labels on some of the items for sale there. This is what she finds:

> packet of sausages — sodium ascorbate, E301
>
> bottle of cola — caramel, E150
>
> tin of soup — monosodium glutamate, E621
>
> tube of toothpaste — titanium dioxide, E171

a)   What does it mean if an additive has an **E number**?

....

....

By searching on the internet, Sue finds that the **E numbers** help explain what the additives do. She summarises the information she finds in a table:

E number of additive	Type of additive
100 to 181	food colourings
300 to 340	antioxidants
620 to 640	flavour enhancers

b)   For each of the items above, use the information in the table to pick the correct reason, A, B, C or D, for the additive being present.

A To change the way the product looks.   **B** To help stop the product going off as quickly.

C To bring out the flavours of the food.   **D** To make it glow in the dark.

i)   Sodium ascorbate in sausages   ....

ii)   Caramel in cola   ....

iii)   Monosodium glutamate in soup   ....

iv)   Titanium dioxide in toothpaste   ....

Food Additives

Q3 Antioxidants are used to help prevent foods '**going off**' as quickly.

a) Which element in the air can be responsible for foods 'going off'? ....

b) Name **two** foods that can be made to stay fresh for longer using antioxidants.

....

Q4 Imran is investigating the effects of different emulsifiers on a mixture of **olive oil** and **water**. He sets up four flasks containing equal amounts of oil and water. He adds nothing else to the first one, and equal amounts of either **additive A**, **B** or **C** to the others. Then he gives them all a good shake and leaves them on a windowsill. After five days he notes their appearance in this table.

Additive used	Appearance after 5 days
None	Oil floating on water. Unpleasant smell.
A	Oil floating on water. No smell.
B	Oil floating on water. Unpleasant smell.
C	Oil and water mixed. Unpleasant smell.

None   A   B   C

a) Which one of the additives is:

i) An antioxidant? ....   **ii)** An emulsifier? ....

b) Justify your answers to part **a)**.

i) ....

ii) ....

c) Why does Imran set up a flask with no additives added?

....

d) Name a food that often contains an emulsifier. ....

Q5 **Lecithin** is added to chocolate drinks in order to prevent the oils separating out from the water. The diagram shows a molecule of lecithin.

a) Label the **hydrophilic** part and the **hydrophobic** part of the lecithin molecule.

b) Briefly explain how this molecule stops the oil and water parts of chocolate drinks from separating into two different layers.

....

....

....

Food Packaging

Q1 Tick the correct boxes to show whether each of the following are examples of **active packaging** or **intelligent packaging**.

active intelligent

a) Cans with 'widgets' to make the drink inside more foamy. ☐ ☐

b) Drinks containers with spots that change colour at different temperatures. ☐ ☐

c) Self-heating and self-cooling drinks cans. ☐ ☐

Q2 Food 'goes off' if it's stored for a long time.

a) Describe why food 'goes off'.

....

....

b) How does drying food help to stop this?

....

c) Describe an active packaging method for fresh food that reduces the amount of water present.

....

Q3 Ali buys some freshly cooked chicken with **intelligent packaging**. She records what the dot on the packaging looks like every 12 hours for three days. Her results are shown in the table.

No. hours since the chicken was bought	0	12	24	36	48	60	72
Appearance of dot	◎	◎	◎	◎	◎	◎	●

a) Describe how this type of intelligent packaging works.

....

....

b) Is this chicken safe to eat after 2 days?

....

Key:

Appearance of dot	Description of food
◎	Very fresh
◎	Still fresh
◎	Still fresh, eat now
●	Not fresh

c) Ali says "All cooked chicken is safe to eat for up to 60 hours." Give two things wrong with this statement.

....

....

Module C1 — Carbon Chemistry

Food Packaging

Q4 Tick the correct boxes to show whether the following statements are **true** or **false**.

Active packaging offers advantages over ordinary food packaging because:

		True	False
a)	It can control its contents.	☐	☐
b)	It allows more food to be squeezed into each packet.	☐	☐
c)	It can make food last longer.	☐	☐
d)	It can reduce the levels of cholesterol we get from foods.	☐	☐

Q5 Julianne took three slices of **bread** (each with exactly the same weight) and sealed them in airtight jars. One jar contained just the bread, one also contained some silica gel and the third contained some fresh orange peel. After a week she estimated the amount of **mould** on each of the slices of bread. The results are shown below.

Contents of jar	% surface of bread with mould
Bread and silica gel	5
Bread only	25
Bread and orange peel	65

Silica gel is a chemical that absorbs water. Fresh orange peel is known to gradually release water.

a) What is Julianne investigating?

....

b) Name one variable she should control in this experiment.

....

c) Why do the jars have to be sealed?

....

d) What can Julianne conclude?

....

Q6 Some cans have **active packaging**.

a) Explain how self-heating cans warm up their contents. ....

....

b) Explain how self-cooling cans cool down their contents. ....

....

Cooking and Chemical Change

Q1   Match the food with the main reason for cooking it.

potatoes

meat

red kidney beans

they are poisonous when raw

to make them easier to digest

to kill microbes that cause disease

Q2   Fill in the blanks in the passage using some of the words in the list below.

protein   cellulose   carbohydrate   heat   digest   swallow   water

Potatoes are a good source of .... Each potato cell is surrounded

by a .... cell wall, which humans can't ....

When the potato is cooked, the .... breaks down the cell wall.

Q3   **Baking powder** contains sodium hydrogencarbonate, $NaHCO_3$, which breaks down when heated.

a)   What is this type of chemical reaction called? ....

b)   **i)**   Name the gas that's released. ....

  ii)   Describe a chemical test for the gas released.

....

....

c)   Write a **word equation** for the breakdown of sodium hydrogencarbonate.

....

d)   Write the **balanced symbol equation** for this reaction.

....

Q4   When meat or eggs are cooked the **protein** molecules they contain are **denatured**.

a)   Explain how cooking causes this chemical change to proteins.

....

....

....

Gas mark 7, licence to grill

b)   Why does denaturing proteins in meat and eggs make them more appealing to eat?

....

8

<u>Perfumes</u>

Q1   New perfumes are sometimes tested on **animals**.

a)   Give one reason **for** testing cosmetic products on animals.

....

b)   Give one reason **against** testing cosmetic products on animals.

....

Q2   A fruity smelling ester can be made by reacting **ethanol** with **ethanoic acid**.

a)   Write a word equation for the **general** reaction used to make an ester.

....

b)   Write numbers in the boxes to put the instructions into the right order for making this ester.

☐	Warm the flask gently on an electric heating plate for 10 minutes.
☐	Put 15 cm³ of ethanoic acid into a 100 cm³ conical flask.
☐	When the flask is cool enough to handle, pour its contents into a 250 cm³ beaker containing 100 cm³ of sodium carbonate solution.
☐	Add 15 cm³ of ethanol and a few drops of concentrated sulfuric acid.
☐	Turn off the heat.

c)   Suggest which of the above steps is carried out to speed up the reaction.

....

d)   What is the purpose of the sodium carbonate solution?

....

Q3   A chemist was asked by an **aftershave company** to make some new scents. Her new compounds were then **tested** to see if they were suitable for use in aftershaves. The results of the tests are summarised in the table.

Liquid	Does it evaporate easily?	Does it dissolve in water?	Does it react with water?
A	yes	no	yes
B	yes	yes	no
C	yes	no	no
D	no	no	no

a)   Which one of these would you use as the scent in an aftershave and why?

....

....

b)   Suggest a further test that should be carried out before the chemical can be used in the aftershave.

....

Module C1 — Carbon Chemistry

Kinetic Theory & Forces Between Particles

Q1 For each description below, say whether it refers to the particles of a **solid**, a **liquid** or a **gas**.

a) There are virtually no forces between particles. ....

b) The particles can vibrate but cannot move from place to place. ....

c) The particles can move around but tend to stick together. ....

d) There are strong forces holding the particles together. ....

e) The particles move freely in straight lines. ....

f) There is no fixed volume or shape. ....

g) There is a fixed volume, but no fixed shape. ....

Q2 Choose from the words in the list to fill in the blanks in this paragraph.

"We wanna be free to do what we wanna do."

speeds	moving	quickly	boiling
evaporation	slowly	attraction	

The particles of a liquid are always .... but there are forces

of .... between them. These forces prevent the particles

moving too far apart. The particles move at different ....

If a particle at the surface is moving .... enough it escapes

the pull from the particles below it. This is ....

Q3 Particles within solids, liquids and gases are constantly moving.

a) How does the volume of a solid change when it is heated? Explain your answer.

....

....

b) How does the pressure of a gas (in a closed container) change when it is heated?
Explain your answer.

....

....

Q4 Fabia is heating some soup. Explain why the smell of soup gets **stronger** as the liquid **warms up**.

....

....

....

Kinetic Theory & Forces Between Particles

Q5   Lucy tested chemicals X, Y and Z to see how suitable they were for use in liquid **air fresheners**.

A volunteer sat at one end of a room and a bottle containing the chemical was opened at the other end. She asked the volunteer to raise a hand when he or she **smelt** the chemical. The time between the bottle being opened and the volunteer's hand being raised was recorded. The test was repeated with different volunteers and the results are shown in the table below.

Chemical	Time (volunteer 1) /s	Time (volunteer 2) /s	Time (volunteer 3) /s	Average time /s
X	45	32	36	
Y	112	98	103	
Z	278	246	243	

a)   Complete the table by working out the **average time** for each of the three chemicals.

b)   Explain why the volunteers didn't smell the chemicals as soon as the bottles were opened.

....

....

....

c)   What does the data tell you about the **volatility** of the chemicals? Circle your answer.

A — Liquid Y is the least volatile chemical.

B — Liquid X is the most volatile chemical.

C — Liquid Z is more volatile than liquid Y.

D — The tests don't tell you anything about volatility.

d)   Suggest two more tests Lucy needs to carry out before any of the chemicals could be used in air fresheners.

....

....

Top Tip: Volatility is just a lovely word describing how easily a liquid evaporates. If a liquid is **volatile**, it evaporates **easily** — and it's likely to have a relatively low boiling point.

Module C1 — Carbon Chemistry

Solutions

Q1   Tick the correct boxes to show whether the following statements are **true** or **false**.

                                                                                                                 True False

a)   A solute is made by dissolving a solid in a liquid.

b)   A solvent is the liquid that the solid is dissolving into.

c)   If a substance is insoluble it will not dissolve in a liquid.

d)   The bonds holding solute molecules together must break before they will dissolve.

Q2   Read the following sentences and list all the **solutes**, **solvents** and **solutions** mentioned.

Salt dissolves in water to form brine. A tincture can be made by dissolving iodine in alcohol.
Gold is soluble in mercury and this mixture is an amalgam.

a)   Solutes ....

b)   Solvents ....

c)   Solutions ....

Q3   Circle the letters of any statements that correctly explain why **nail varnish** won't dissolve in **water**.

> **A**   Water is not a good solvent.

> **B**   The forces between the molecules of nail varnish are stronger than those between the molecules of water and the molecules of nail varnish.

> **C**   Water is only good for dissolving substances that are non-toxic.

> **D**   The forces between the molecules of water are stronger than those between the molecules of water and the molecules of nail varnish.

Q4   Neena is investigating the **solubility** of sodium chloride in water. She takes **10 g** of the compound and adds it to **10 cm³** of water. After stirring for a few minutes there is some sodium chloride that won't dissolve. Neena filters the solution and lets the leftover solid dry. The solid weighs **6.8 g**.

a)   Calculate the mass of sodium chloride that dissolved in 10 cm³ of water.   ....

Neena repeats the experiment using **methanol** instead of water.
She finds that only **0.1 g** of sodium chloride will dissolve in 10 cm³ of methanol.

b)   Write a conclusion for this experiment.

....

Q5   I have got blue ink all over my cat (long story) and it **won't** wash off with water. Give two important properties I should think about when choosing a suitable **solvent** to remove the ink.

1. ....

2. ....

Module C1 — Carbon Chemistry

Polymers

Q1 Tick the box next to the **true** statement below.

☐ The monomer of polyethene is ethene.

☐ The polymer of polyethene is ethane.

☐ The monomer of polyethene is ethane.

We bring you gold, frankincense...
and poly-myrrh

Q2 **Addition polymers** are formed when **unsaturated monomers** link together.

a) What is an unsaturated compound?

....

b) Name two conditions needed to make addition polymers.

....

Q3 The equation below shows the polymerisation of ethene to form **polyethene**.

$$n \left(\begin{array}{c} H \quad H \\ | \quad\ | \\ C = C \\ | \quad\ | \\ H \quad H \end{array} \right) \longrightarrow \left(\begin{array}{c} H \quad H \\ | \quad\ | \\ -C - C- \\ | \quad\ | \\ H \quad H \end{array} \right)_n$$

many ethene
molecules

polyethene

a) Draw a similar diagram in the box below to show the polymerisation of **propene** (C_3H_6).

It's easier if
you think of
propene as:
$$\begin{array}{c} H \quad H \\ | \quad\ | \\ C = C \\ | \quad\ | \\ H \quad CH_3 \end{array}$$

b) Name the polymer you have drawn. ....

Q4 Nigel has two rulers made from **different plastics**. He first tries to bend them and then he heats them. The results are shown in the table.

	RESULT ON BENDING	RESULT ON HEATING
Ruler 1	Ruler bends easily and springs back into shape	Ruler becomes soft and then melts
Ruler 2	Ruler snaps in two	Ruler doesn't soften and eventually turns black

a) Which ruler is made from a polymer that has strong forces between its molecules? ....

b) Explain why the other type of plastic melts and bends more easily.

....

....

Polymers and Their Uses

Q1   From the list below, underline any **properties** you think it is important for a plastic to have if it is to be used to make **Wellington boots**.

N.B. Chlorine dissolves lycra

low melting point   waterproof   rigid   lightweight   heat-resistant

Q2   Complete the table to show the most suitable **use** of each polymer using the options in the list.

carrier bags   kettles   window frames   disposable cups

Each use can only be used once.

POLYMER	PROPERTIES	USE
polypropene	heat-resistant	
polystyrene foam	thermal insulator	
low density polyethene	lightweight	
PVC	strong, durable, rigid	

Q3   Suggest a **problem** with each of the following methods of **disposing plastics**.

a)   Burial in landfill sites. ....

....

b)   Burning. ....

....

c)   Recycling. ....

....

Q4   Kate has three black jackets. One is made from **nylon**, another from nylon coated with **polyurethane**, and the third from a type of breathable fabric called **GORE-TEX®**.

a)   Explain why the jacket coated with polyurethane would be better for Kate to wear on a rainy day than the plain nylon jacket.

....

b)   Which of the jackets would you advise Kate to take for a week's hiking in Wales?
Explain your answer.

....

....

c)   The **GORE-TEX®** jacket is made from a thin film of another plastic called **expanded PTFE** laminated onto a layer of **nylon**. Explain how the two work together to give the material its useful properties.

....

....

....

Alkanes and Alkenes

Q1   Tick the boxes to show whether the following are **true** or **false**.

                                                                         True False

a)   Alkenes have double bonds between the hydrogen atoms.   ☐ ☐

b)   Alkenes are unsaturated.   ☐ ☐

c)   Alkanes won't form polymers.   ☐ ☐

d)   Alkanes tend to burn with a smoky flame.   ☐ ☐

e)   Alkanes decolourise bromine water.   ☐ ☐

Q2   Hydrocarbons are held together with **covalent** bonds.

a)   Are these statements about covalent bonds **true** or **false**?

                                                                                     True False

   i)   Covalent bonds form when electrons are transferred from one atom to another.   ☐ ☐

   ii) Covalent bonds form between atoms so that both have a full outer shell of electrons.   ☐ ☐

   iii) Atoms can be joined by single or double covalent bonds.   ☐ ☐

   iv) All molecules that contain covalent bonds will decolourise bromine water.   ☐ ☐

b)   How many covalent bonds do the following atoms make?

   i) Carbon ....   ii) Hydrogen ....

Q3   The general formula for **alkanes** is C_nH_{2n+2}. Use this to write down the formulas of these alkanes.

a)   pentane (5 carbons) ....   **b)**   hexane (6 carbons) ....

c)   octane (8 carbons) ....   **d)**   dodecane (12 carbons) ....

Q4   Complete this table showing the **molecular** and **displayed** formulas of some alkenes.

Alkene	Formula	Displayed formula
Ethene	a)	b)
c)	C_3H_6	d)
Butene	e)	$\begin{array}{c} H \\ H \end{array}\!\!\!C{=}C{-}C{-}C{-}H$ (with H atoms on each carbon)

Q5   Using a chemical test, describe how you could tell **hexane** and **hexene** apart.

....

....

Fractional Distillation of Crude Oil

Q1   Circle the correct answer to each of the following questions.

a)   Why is crude oil called a fossil fuel?

A — Because the oil is millions of years old.

B — Because the oil was formed from animals and plants buried long ago.

C — Because burning the fuel causes global warming.

b)   Why is crude oil non-renewable?

A — It is impossible to create new oil.

B — Oil is very hard to find.

C — Oil takes many millions of years to form.

phwoar... nice tank, love

Q2   Circle the correct words to complete these sentences.

a)   Crude oil is a **mixture** / **compound** of different molecules.

b)   The molecules in crude oil are all **hydrocarbons** / **carbohydrates**.

c)   If crude oil were heated, the **first** / **last** fraction to be obtained would be bitumen.

d)   Diesel has **larger** / **smaller** molecules than petrol.

Q3   Label this diagram of a **fractionating column** to show where these substances can be collected.

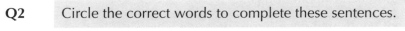

petrol   kerosene   diesel   oil   bitumen

These are in order of molecule size, with the smallest on the left.

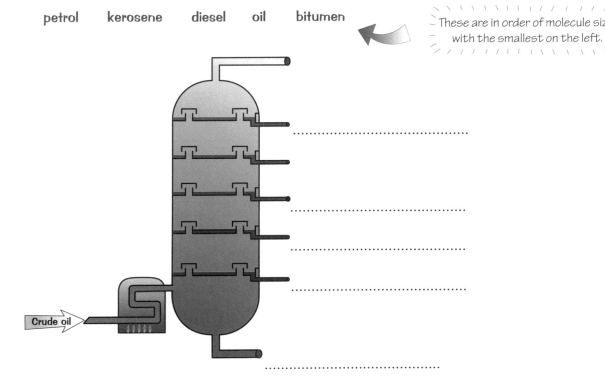

Crude oil

....

....

....

....

....

Fractional Distillation of Crude Oil

Q4 Crude oil is separated into different **fractions** by boiling.

a) Put these crude oil fractions into order from highest to lowest boiling point.

diesel	naphtha	kerosene	petrol

highest .... lowest

b) Put the same fractions in order from most to least carbon atoms in their molecules.

most .... least

c) Look at your answers for parts **a)** and **b)**. What is the connection between the number of carbon atoms in a molecule and its boiling point?

....

....

Q5 The following sentences describe how crude oil is separated by **fractional distillation**. Fill in the blanks in the following sentences using some of the words below.

high   gases   cooler   heated   smaller   low   bottom   hotter   fractions

A Crude oil is .... causing most of the hydrocarbons to boil.

B The hot .... rise up the fractionating column.

C As they rise, the temperature begins to get ....

D Near the .... of the column, large molecules with lots of carbon atoms condense first because they have .... boiling points.

E As the gases rise further and become cooler, ... molecules with lower boiling points turn into liquids.

F In this way crude oil is separated into ...., which are mixtures of only a few different molecules, all with similar numbers of carbon atoms and similar boiling points.

Top Tip: Fractional distillation can be a tricky idea to get your head round, but once you do you'll be able to answer anything they throw at you. Learn the order of the fractions too, they love that.

Hydrocarbon Properties — Bonds

Q1 **Pentane** contains **5** carbon atoms, whereas **decane** has **10** carbon atoms.
Give **three** differences between the physical properties of pentane and decane.

1. ....

2. ....

3. ....

Q2 Here is a table showing the properties of some **alkanes**.

Alkane	Melting point (°C)	Boiling point (°C)
Methane (CH_4)	−182	−162
Pentane (C_5H_{12})	−130	36
Hexane (C_6H_{14})	−95	69
Decane ($C_{10}H_{22}$)	−30	174
Octadecane ($C_{18}H_{38}$)	28	317

a) Which of these alkanes are liquids at room temperature (25 °C)?

....

b) Which of these liquids is the most volatile? ....

c) Which alkane will be a solid at room temperature? ....

d) Which of the liquids will flow most easily along a pipe? ....

Q3 Jim investigated how the **size** of a hydrocarbon molecule affects its **volatility**. He took 50 cm³ of each of three different hydrocarbons and put them into evaporating basins. He left them for five hours and then measured how much of each was left. His results are shown in the table below.

No. of C atoms	Initial vol. (cm³)	Vol. after 5 hours (cm³)	Vol. lost (cm³)
6	50	8	
10	50	37	
12	50	48	

a) Complete the table by filling in the volume of each hydrocarbon that has evaporated.

b) If this is to be a fair test, what must be kept the same for all three hydrocarbons (apart from using the same volume of each)?

Think what could affect how fast the liquids evaporate.

....

c) What can Jim conclude about volatility and the size of hydrocarbons?

....

Q4 Explain the trend in the boiling points of alkanes in terms of **intermolecular forces**.

....

....

....

Cracking

Q1 Fill in the gaps using the words below.

| high | shorter | longer | catalyst | cracking | diesel | low | molecules | petrol |

There is more need for .... chain fractions of crude oil such

as .... than for .... chain fractions such as

.... Heating long hydrocarbon molecules to

.... temperatures with a .... breaks them down

into smaller .... This is called ....

Q2 Circle the correct answer for each of the following questions.

a) What type of chemical reaction is cracking?

A — Neutralisation　　**B** — Displacement

C — Thermal decomposition　　**D** — Redox

b) Why are high temperatures needed to crack alkanes?

A — Catalysts only work when hot.　　**B** — Energy is needed to break strong covalent bonds.

C — Large alkane molecules have strong intermolecular forces.

D — Alkenes are very unreactive hydrocarbons.

Q3 Cracking produces different types of **useful molecules**.

a) Name the two types of molecule you get from cracking a long-chain hydrocarbon.

....

b) A molecule produced in the cracking process has the formula C_2H_4.

i) What is the name of this hydrocarbon? ....

ii) What is the main use of C_2H_4? ....

c) Name two conditions needed to crack liquid paraffin in the lab.

....

Top Tips: Cracking is really useful, and dead important too. It helps us get the most out of crude oil, so we don't end up with loads of a fraction that we don't want or need. Hooray for cracking!

Cracking

Q4 Change this diagram into a **word equation** and a **symbol equation**.

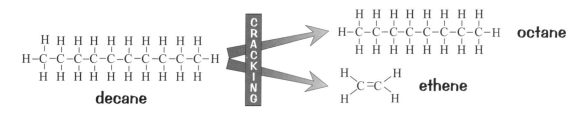

a) Word equation: .... → .... + ...

b) Symbol equation: .... → .... + ...

Q5 Horatio owns a **crude oil refinery**. He records the amount of each fraction that's **present** in a sample of crude oil and compares it against how much of each fraction his customers want.

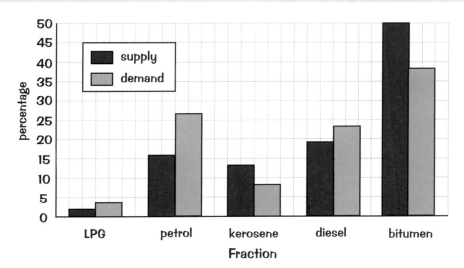

a) Which fractions in this sample of crude oil are in excess (more is produced than can be sold)?

....

b) For which fraction in this sample does the demand outweigh the supply by the greatest amount?

....

c) Explain how cracking will help Horatio match the levels of supply to the levels of demand.

....

....

d) Suggest how else cracking can benefit crude oil companies economically.

....

....

Fuels from Crude Oil

Q1   Describe the **environmental problems** associated with each of the following:

  a) **Transporting** crude oil across the sea in tankers. ....

....

  b) **Burning** oil products to release the energy they contain. ....

....

Q2   Circle the correct words to complete the passage below.

> We rely on crude oil to provide us with **energy / metals** and as a source of raw materials for
>
> making chemicals. Because crude oil is a **renewable / non-renewable** resource it will eventually
>
> run out. As it becomes scarcer the price of oil will **increase / decrease** and everything that
>
> relies on oil as a raw material or fuel for its production will become **more expensive / cheaper**.

Q3   Crude oil is used for many different **purposes**.

  a) Give three fractions from crude oil that are used as fuels.

....

  b) Why should we try to conserve energy and recycle plastics as much as possible?

....

....

Q4   Isobella is trying to decide which hydrocarbon, A or B, is the best one to use as a fuel.
She tests the **energy content** of the hydrocarbons by using them to heat 50 cm³ of water
from 25 °C to 40 °C. The results of this experiment are shown in the table.

Hydrocarbon	Initial Mass (g)	Final Mass (g)	Mass of Fuel Burnt (g)
A	98	92	
B	102	89	

Today's Lecture:
'My favourite few Ls'

  a) Complete the table by calculating the mass of fuel that was burned in each case.

  b) Which fuel contains more energy per gram? ....

  c) Name four other things Isobella should consider when choosing the best fuel to use.

....

....

Burning Fuels

Q1 Which of the following statements are **true** when burning
a hydrocarbon **incompletely**? Circle the correct answers.

A — It produces a smoky flame.

B — It burns with a blue flame.

C — It produces carbon dioxide.

E — There is plenty of ventilation.

D — It produces carbon monoxide.

Q2 Hydrocarbons make good **fuels**.

a) What is a fuel? ....

b) Write a **general word equation** for completely burning a hydrocarbon in the open air.

....

c) Write **balanced symbol equations** for completely burning these alkanes in open air:

i) methane, CH_4 ....

ii) propane, C_3H_8 ....

Q3 **Incomplete combustion** can cause problems.

a) Why is it important to regularly service gas appliances? ....

....

b) Which releases more energy:

i) complete or incomplete combustion? ....

ii) a blue flame or a yellow flame? Explain your answer. ....

....

c) Complete the balanced symbol equation for the incomplete combustion of butane.

C_4H_{10} + ... → .... H_2O + ... CO_2 + ... + ...

Q4 Describe how the apparatus on the right could be used
to show that water and carbon dioxide are produced
when **hexane** (a hydrocarbon) is completely burned.

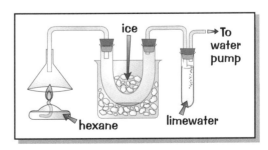

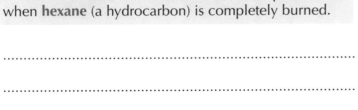

....

....

....

....

Energy Transfer in Reactions

Q1 Use the words to **complete** the passage below. (Each word can be used more than once.)

| endothermic | exothermic | energy | heat | an increase | a decrease |

All chemical reactions involve changes in ....

In .... reactions, ... energy is given out to the surroundings.

A thermometer will show .... in temperature.

In .... reactions, ... energy is taken in from the

surroundings. A thermometer will show .... in temperature.

Q2 Fiz investigated the **temperature change** during a reaction. She added 25 cm³ of sodium hydroxide solution to 25 cm³ of hydrochloric acid. She used a **data logger** to measure the temperature of the reaction over the first **five** seconds.

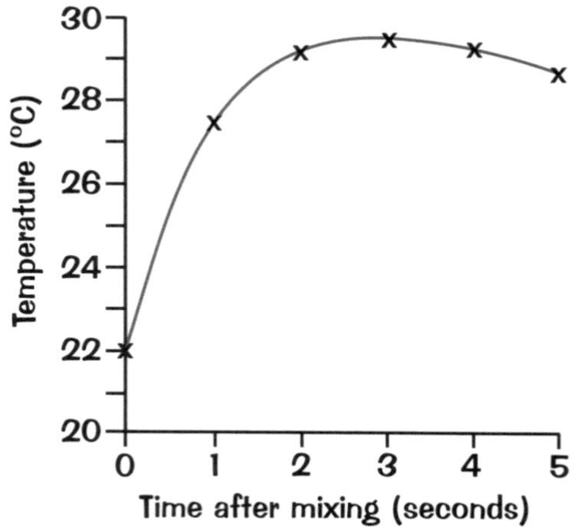

Fiz plotted her results on the graph shown.

a) What was the increase in temperature due to the reaction?

....

b) Circle any of the words below that correctly describe the reaction in this experiment.

neutralisation   combustion

endothermic   respiration   exothermic

c) Why is it difficult to get **an accurate result** for the temperature change in an experiment like this?

....

Q3 **Circle** the correct words to complete each of the sentences below.

a) An example of an endothermic reaction is **photosynthesis / combustion**.

b) An example of an exothermic reaction is **photosynthesis / neutralisation**.

c) Bond breaking is an **exothermic / endothermic** process.

d) Bond forming is an **exothermic / endothermic** process.

Q4 During the following reaction the reaction mixture's temperature **increases**.

A B + C ➡ A C + B

a) Is the reaction exothermic or endothermic? ....

b) Which bond is stronger, A–B or A–C? Explain your answer.

....

Measuring the Energy Content of Fuels

Q1 Write down the formulas for calculating:

a) the energy transferred to water during a calorimetric experiment.

....

b) the energy output of a fuel per gram.

....

Q2 Ross wants to compare the **energy content** of two fuels, petrol and a petrol alternative, fuel X.

a) Draw a labelled diagram in the box to show the apparatus Ross could use for comparing the energy content of these two fuels in a simple calorimetric experiment.

b) Name **two variables** that Ross has to **control** to ensure a fair test when using this method.

....

c) He finds that **0.7 g** of petrol raises the temperature of **50 g** of water by **30.5 °C**.

i) Calculate the energy gained by the water.

....

ii) Use your answer to **i)** to calculate the energy produced per gram of petrol.
Give your answer in units of **kJ/g**.

....

d) Burning **0.8 g** of fuel X raises the temperature of **50 g** of water by **27 °C**.

Calculate the energy produced per gram of fuel X.

....

....

e) Using this evidence only, decide whether petrol or fuel X would make the better fuel.
Explain your choice.

....

Module C1 — Carbon Chemistry

Mixed Questions — Module C1

Q1 A packet of ham contains an **antioxidant**, E310. Inside the packaging there is a sachet of **silica**.

a) Both these things help to make the ham last longer. Explain how each does this.

i) E310 ....

....

ii) Silica ....

....

b) Suggest why there is more demand for long-lasting products today than there was 50 years ago.

....

....

Q2 **Baking powder** is often one of the ingredients in cakes.

a) Name the chemical that baking powder contains. ....

b) Explain why this chemical is a useful addition to a cake mix.

....

....

c) The cake mix fills the bottom of the tin that it is poured into, but when cooked, the cake no longer flows. Explain why this is in terms of the **movement** of the particles and the **forces** between them.

....

....

d) Are the chemical changes that take place when a cake is baked **reversible** or **irreversible**?

....

Q3 **Chloroethene** (C_2H_3Cl) is used to make the addition polymer, **polychloroethene** (PVC).

a) What feature does chloroethene have that allows it to form an addition polymer?

....

b) Write an equation in the space on the right for the polymerisation of chloroethene, using **displayed formulae** to show the structure of chloroethene and the repeating unit in PVC.

c) PVC is a widely used plastic. Give a use for PVC. ....

d) PVC is **non-biodegradable**. What does this mean? ....

....

Mixed Questions — Module C1

Q4   Nail varnish does **not** dissolve in water. This is important, otherwise every time a person washed their hands it would wash away.

a)   Explain, in terms of the molecules, why nail varnish does not dissolve in water.

    ....

b)   Explain, in terms of the molecules, how nail varnish remover removes the varnish.

    ....

c)   The active chemical in nail varnish is a **volatile liquid**.

    i)   Explain what "**volatile**" means.

        ....

    ii)   Explain, in terms of the particles, what happens when this chemical **evaporates** from the nails.

        ....

        ....

    iii)   Name **another product** that must be **volatile** in order to work effectively. Explain why this is.

        ....

        ....

Q5   **30 g** of a fuel, X, is burnt and used to heat **100 g** of water. The temperature of the water before heating was **20 °C**, and after heating it was **42 °C**.

The specific heat capacity of water = 4.2

a)   Calculate the energy transferred per gram of this fuel.

    ....

    ....

b)   What name is given to a reaction like this one that gives out energy? ....

c)   Which quantity of energy is the larger in this reaction? Underline the correct answer.

        The energy required to break the old bonds   **The energy released in forming the new bonds.**

d)   Give another property of this fuel, other than its energy value, that should be taken into account when deciding whether or not to use it industrially.

    ....

e)   Fuel X contains only hydrogen and carbon. What could the products of the reaction include when fuel X is burnt:

    i)   in plentiful oxygen ....

    ii)   in low oxygen ....

Module C1 — Carbon Chemistry

Mixed Questions — Module C1

Q6 Crude oil is a mixture of hydrocarbons, which is separated by **fractional distillation** into useful fractions.

Refinery gas (bottled gas)

Petrol

....

Kerosene

....

Oil

Crude oil

Bitumen

a) i) Label the **diesel** and **naphtha** fractions on the diagram.

ii) Which fraction has the higher boiling point?
Underline the correct answer.

naphtha   diesel

iii) Why does this fraction have a higher boiling point?

....

....

b) Explain how the fractions are separated in fractional distillation.

....

....

c) Explain why plastic products may become much more expensive in the future.

....

....

Q7 **Cracking** is an important process used to turn long-chain hydrocarbons into shorter molecules.

a) Explain why this process is so important.

....

....

b) Give the industrial conditions usually used for cracking.

....

c) Dodecane ($C_{12}H_{26}$) is a long-chain hydrocarbon found in the naphtha fraction.

i) Write a balanced equation for cracking dodecane to form octane and ethene.

....

ii) Circle the words that describe ethene molecules.

saturated   hydrocarbon   ester   unsaturated   alkene   alkane   polymer

iii) Ethene has a **double bond** between its carbon atoms, but octane contains only **single bonds**.
Explain the difference between these two types of bond.

....

....

Paints and Pigments

Q1   Match each term on the left with the correct meaning on the right.

pigment   holds pigment particles to a surface

colloid   keeps paint runny

solvent   tiny particles dispersed in another material

binding medium   gives paint its colour

Q2   Circle the correct words to complete the sentences below.

a)   Gloss paints are **oil-based** / **water-based**. Emulsion paints are **oil-based** / **water-based**.

b)   Paint dries as the **solvent** / **binding medium** evaporates.

c)   In oil-based paints the solvent is **oil** / **something that dissolves oil**.

Q3   A DIY shop sells both **water-based** and **oil-based** paint.

a)   i)   Which of these types of paint is more likely to be harmful if used **indoors**?   _Oil-based_

     ii) Explain why this is and suggest a **safety precaution** you should take.
         It release's toxic gasses. You should use
         it in venilated areas.

b)   This pie chart shows how the paint sold in the DIY shop is **used**.
      Do you think that more water-based or oil-based paint is sold?
      Explain your answer. 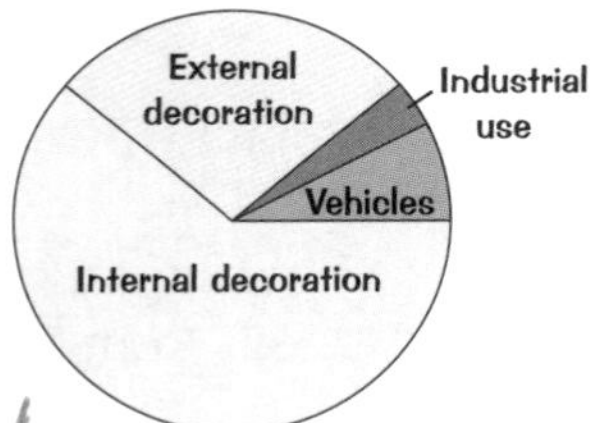
      water based because it is safer
      indoors, and the internal paint is used more.

      External decoration   Industrial use
      Vehicles
      Internal decoration

Q4   Which of the following statements are **true** and which are **false**?

		True	False
a)	Oil-based paints dry quicker than emulsion paints.		✓
b)	The particles in colloids are always solids.		✓
c)	Emulsion paints usually use polymers as binding materials.	✓	
d)	The particles in colloids are so small that they stay dispersed and do not settle.	✓	

Q5   Imagine it is your job to develop a paint that can be used in **space**.

a)   Why would traditional oil-based paints not be suitable here?
      Needs oxygen to dry it.

      Hint: There's no oxygen in space.

b)   Why would the paint have to be very sticky?

Dyes and Special Pigments

Q1 Choose from the words below to complete the paragraphs.

phosphorescent	indigo	thermochromic	synthetic	natural	purple

Before 1856, dyes were only made from ......*natural*...... sources.

For example, ...*indigo*...... dye came from a plant and ......*purple*...... dye came from a rare sea snail. When ......*synthetic*...... dyes were invented, the range of colours available increased.

Now, ...*thermochromic*...... pigments can be produced that change colour when heated.

Also, ...*phosphorescent*...... pigments that glow in the dark are available.

Q2 Join each statement to the **type of pigment** it relates to.

can become transparent
when heated

used in thermometers

used in emergency exit signs

glow in the dark

PHOSPHORESCENT PIGMENTS

THERMOCHROMIC PIGMENTS

used in road signs

used in kettles that change
colour when they boil

store light energy

Q3 The diagram shows two watches with **glow-in-the-dark hands**. One is from **1950**, the other is from **2006**.

1950   2006

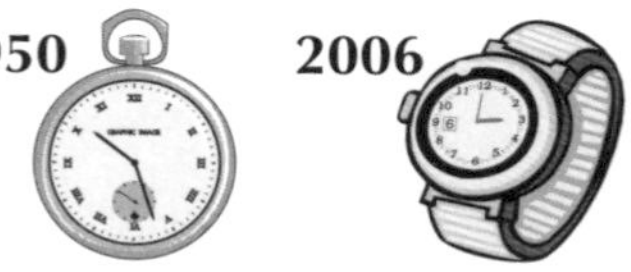

a) What type of paint was probably used on the hands of the watch from:

   i) 1950? ....

   ii) 2006? ....

b) Explain why the type of paint used was changed. ....

   ....

Q4 **Thermochromic pigments** are used for novelty purposes, for example on mugs and T-shirts.

   Describe **two non-novelty** uses of themochromic pigments.

   1) Acrylic paint, changes colour

   ....

Module C2 — Rocks and Metals

Construction Materials

Q1 Match each **construction material** to the **raw materials** that are needed to make it.

CONSTRUCTION MATERIALS   **RAW MATERIALS**

cement   ores
bricks   limestone
iron   sand
aluminium   clay
concrete   gravel

Some construction materials are made from more than one raw material from the list.

Q2 Choose from the words below to complete the paragraphs.

| clay | sodium carbonate | cement | calcium carbonate | silicon dioxide |
| melting | extracting | aluminium | fired | bricks | soda |

a) Glass is made by _melting_ limestone (_calcium carbonate_), sand (_silicon dioxide_) and soda (_sodium carbonate_), then cooling the mixture.

b) When moist, _clay_ is a mouldable material made from decomposed rock. If it is _fired_ at high temperature it can made into _bricks_ .

c) Powdered limestone can also be mixed with _clay_ , then roasted in a kiln to make _cement_ .

Q3 Reinforced concrete is called a '**composite material**'.

a) Explain why this is. ....

b) Give an advantage that reinforced concrete has over normal concrete.

....

Q4 Quarrying limestone can cause a variety of **problems**.

a) Describe **three environmental problems** caused by quarrying.

1. _Destroys habitats_

2. _Noise & pollution_

3. _dust_

b) Explain why the **closure** of a quarry may be a cause of concern for local residents.

Bg it can turn into lakes, people may fall in and drown.

Module C2 — Rocks and Metals

<u>Extracting Pure Copper</u>

Q1 Copper is found in the ground in **ores** such as **malachite**.

a) Suggest how copper could be **extracted** from malachite? *Electrolysis*

b) Why might this extracted copper need to be **purified**?

So it conducts better

c) What is used as the **anode** during the purification of copper by electrolysis? *Impure copper*

d) Explain why pure copper ends up at the **cathode** during electrolysis.

....

....

....

Q2 Write **half-equations** for the purifying of copper by electrolysis.

Cathode: ....

Anode: ....

Q3 Tick the boxes to show which of the following are good reasons for **recycling copper**.

[✓] It's cheaper than mining new copper. [✓] It uses less energy and therefore less fossil fuel.

[ ] You obtain a higher quality of copper. [ ] Less carbon dioxide is produced as a result.

Q4 During the purification of copper the **impure sludge** simply falls to the bottom. It does **not** follow the copper ions to the cathode. Why do you think this is?

The copper ions that leave the anode are positively charged.

Not pure metal.

....

Q5 Silver can be purified in the same way as copper. Write **half-equations** for the processes that take place at the anode and the cathode.

Silver only loses one electron to become a silver ion.

Cathode: $Cu^2 + 2e^- \rightarrow Cu$

Anode: $Cu \rightarrow Cu^2 + 2e^-$

Q6 Suppose the electrolysis of **copper** was carried out using an electrolyte that contained **zinc** ions instead of copper ions. Why would this **not** be a good idea? Underline the correct answer.

The zinc ions will not conduct an electric current.

The copper produced will have zinc impurities in it.

A poisonous gas would be produced.

<u>The zinc and copper ions will react with each other.</u>

Alloys

Q1   Choose from the words below to complete the paragraph.

| sulfur | carbon | bronze | non-metal | alloy | brass | gas |

If you mix a metal with another element the resulting mixture is called an

...........Alloy........... . The other element may be a ....Non metal. .

An example of this is steel where iron is mixed with small amounts of

.......Carbon....... . Alternatively, the other element could be another metal.

An example of this is .....brass..... where copper is combined with zinc.

Q2   Metals are mixed with other elements to give them different properties for different uses.

a)   Tick the correct boxes to show whether each statement is **true** or **false**.

	True	False
i) Bronze is made of copper and tin.	☑	☐
ii) Steel contains copper.	☐	☑
iii) Nitinol is made of silver and nickel.	☐	☑
iv) Amalgam contains mercury.	☑	☐
v) Brass contains zinc.	☑	☐
vi) Solder contains aluminium.	☐	☑
vii) Brass contains carbon.	☐	☑

b)   Draw lines to join up the following alloys with their uses.

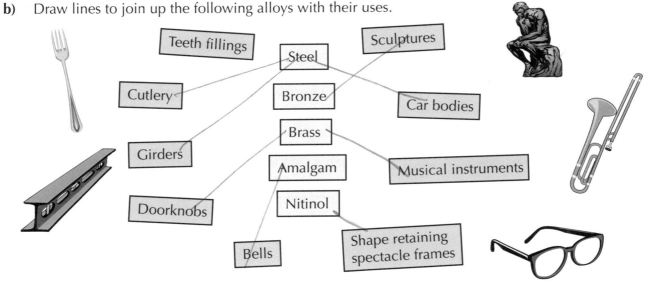

Teeth fillings   Steel   Sculptures

Cutlery   Bronze   Car bodies

Girders   Brass

Doorknobs   Amalgam   Musical instruments

Nitinol

Bells   Shape retaining spectacle frames

Alloys

Q3 The table below shows three types of **bronze** alloy. These alloys only contain tin and copper.

a) Circle the correct words in each pair to complete the passage below.

Bronze is much **softer** / **harder** and **stronger** / **weaker** than tin.
It's also **more** / **less** resistant to corrosion than either copper or tin.

b) What is the % of copper in **commercial bronze**?
.... 90%

c) What type of bronze do you think is most likely to be used for gold decorations?
...Hi-copper bronze...

Alloy	% tin	% copper	Appearance
Hi-Tin Bronze	20	80	Silver
Commercial bronze	10		Dark orange
Hi-copper bronze	5	95	Gold

Q4 Different alloys have different **advantages** and **disadvantages**.

a) Give one disadvantage of **quick-solidifying solder**.

....

b) If you could make car bodies from **nitinol**, what advantage would this have?

....

....

Think about how easy it would be to repair after a minor crash?

c) What physical property makes a **brass** screw better than a copper screw?

....

d) Why are you much more likely to see an outdoor sculpture made of **bronze** than of copper or tin?

....

e) What property of steel makes it more suitable than iron for:

i) drill bits. ....

ii) ships. ....

__Top Tips:__ The properties of an alloy determine what it's used for, e.g. if you want an alloy that's strong, but lightweight and will harden over time, then a great solution is duralumin (which is aluminium with 4% copper, 1% manganese and some magnesium).

Building Cars

Q1 Use the words below to complete the paragraph.

salty iron reduction oxidation iron(II) oxide iron(III) oxide rusting water

.... is the corrosion of .... If unprotected iron

comes into contact with oxygen and ...., a chemical reaction happens.

Oxygen reacts with iron to produce hydrated ...., also known as rust.

This is known as an .... reaction. This reaction is speeded up if

the water is acidic or ....

Q2 In the table below list an advantage and a disadvantage of using **aluminium** and **steel** to make car bodies.

	Steel	**Aluminium**
Advantage		
Disadvantage		

Q3 Fill in the missing labels on the diagram using the words and phrases below. You don't have to use all the words and phrases.

Materials:
Plastic
Copper
Glass
Iron
Natural and synthetic fibres

Advantages:
Light and hardwearing
Strong, easily welded
Electrical conductor
Transparent

Dashboard
Material:
Advantage:

Windows
Material:
Advantage:

Seats
Material:
Advantage:

Electrical wiring
Material:
Advantage:

Q4 Which of the following statements are **true** and which are **false**?

		True	False
a)	Cars are recycled to save natural resources and to reduce landfill use.	☐	☐
b)	There are no laws stating how much of a new car must be recyclable.	☐	☐
c)	It's easy to separate out the non-metal bits of a car.	☐	☐
d)	Currently, scrap metal is the main component of cars that is recycled.	☐	☐

The Three Different Types of Rock

Q1   Join up each **rock type** with the correct **method of formation** and an **example**.

ROCK TYPE   METHOD OF FORMATION   EXAMPLE

| igneous rocks | formed from layers of sediment | granite |

| metamorphic rocks | formed when magma cools | limestone |

| sedimentary rocks | formed under intense heat and pressure | marble |

Q2   Circle the correct words to complete the passage below.

Metamorphic / Igneous rock is formed when magma pushes up into (or through) the

crust / mantle and cools.

If the magma cools before it reaches the surface it will cool **slowly / quickly**, forming

big / small crystals. This rock is known as **extrusive / intrusive** igneous rock.

Examples of this are **basalt / granite** and **gabbro / rhyolite**.

However the magma that reaches the surface will cool **slowly / quickly**, forming

big / small crystals. This rock is known as **extrusive / intrusive** igneous rock.

Examples of this are **basalt / granite** and **gabbro / rhyolite**.

Q3   Erica notices that the stonework of her local church contains tiny fragments of **sea shells**.

a)   Suggest an explanation for this.

....

....

b)   Describe how sedimentary rock is 'cemented' together.

....

....

c)   Powdered limestone and powdered marble react with other chemicals, such as hydrochloric acid, in an identical fashion. Explain this.

....

Top Tips: You might think that rocks are just boring lumps of.... rock. But you'd be wrong — rocks are actually boring lumps of different kinds of rock. And the kind of rock they are depends on how they're formed — and this is the stuff you need to make sure you know.

The Three Different Types of Rock

Q4 Use the words below to complete the paragraph.

| heat | metamorphic | igneous | crystals | texture | magma | sedimentary |

.... rock forms from layers of sediment compacted at the bottom of

seas or lakes over millions of years. As layers build up, the older rock is subjected to

.... and pressure. This can change the ....

and mineral structure of the rock and is how .... rocks form.

If the rock gets too hot it melts and is then known as ....

This can force its way to the surface and cool to become .... rock.

These rocks contain minerals in the form of ....

Q5 Below are the processes involved in the formation of **marble**.

a) Number the boxes to show the order in which they occur.

☐ Heat and pressure causes limestone to change into marble.

☐ Dead sea creatures become buried in sediment.

☐ Sea creatures die.

☐ Natural mineral cement sticks the sediment together and limestone forms.

☐ Several layers of sediment build up and compress the lower layers.

b) Describe the **differences** between limestone and marble.

....

....

Q6 Calcium carbonate can undergo **thermal decomposition**.

a) Explain what thermal decomposition means.

....

....

b) Write out the word and symbol equations for the thermal decomposition of calcium carbonate.

Word equation: ....

Symbol equation: ....

The Earth's Structure

Q1   Look at the diagram showing the boundary between the African and Arabian plates.

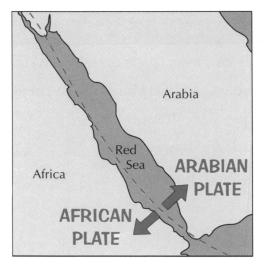

The Red Sea is widening at a speed of 1.6 cm per year.

Remember to include a unit in your answer.

a)   If the sea level remains the same, how much will the Red Sea widen in 10 000 years?

....

b)   The Red Sea is currently exactly 325 km wide at a certain point. If the sea level remains the same, how wide will the Red Sea be at this point in 20 000 years' time?

....

....

Don't forget to make sure your distances are in the same unit.

Q2   The map below on the left shows where most of the world's earthquakes take place.

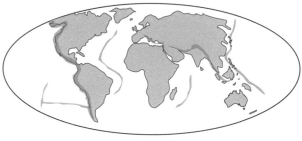 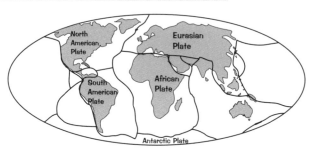

= main earthquake zones

Compare this map to the one showing the tectonic plates.
What do you notice about the main earthquake zones?

....

....

Module C2 — Rocks and Metals

The Earth's Structure

Q3 Draw a simple diagram of the Earth's structure.
Label the **crust**, **mantle** and **core** and write a brief description of each.

Q4 Match up the description to the key phrase or word.

Lithosphere	Hot spots that often sit on plate boundaries
Continental crust	A well-known plate boundary in North America
Convection current	Caused by sudden movements of plates
Tectonic plates	Made up of a 'jigsaw' of plates
Eurasian Plate	Caused largely by radioactive decay within the Earth
Earthquakes	Large pieces of crust and upper mantle
Volcanoes	A thin layer of rock forming most of the land
San Andreas Fault	Moving away from the North American Plate but toward the African Plate

Q5 Jo says, "The Earth was molten when it formed — that's the reason why it is still hot at its centre."

a) Is Jo right? Explain your answer.

....

b) **i)** Which part of the Earth does the magnetic field originate from? ....

ii) What elements make up this part of the Earth? ....

iii) Is this part of the Earth solid or liquid? ....

Top Tips: So, let's get this straight — we're aboard a large rocky raft, which is floating on a huge almost ball-shaped thing, that's spinning through space. Sounds perfectly reasonable... hmmm.

Evidence for Plate Tectonics

Q1   Use the words below to complete the paragraph.

continents   Sangria   evolution   living creatures
fast-food restaurants   plate tectonics   fossils   Pangaea

All the continents were once joined in a huge land mass called ....

We now believe this land mass slowly split up to form the ....

This is the theory of .... It explains why continents thousands

of miles apart have identical .... and

....

Q2   Fossils of the prehistoric fern **Glossopteris** have been found
in India, Australia, Africa, South America and Antarctica.

   a)   Explain why this distribution cannot be accounted for by seed dispersal.

....

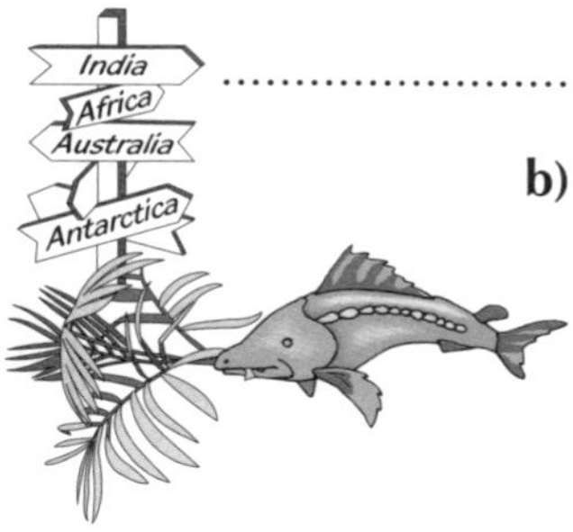

   b)   What would be a better explanation for the fern's distribution?

....

....

Q3   The diagram below shows rock sequences from four different continents.

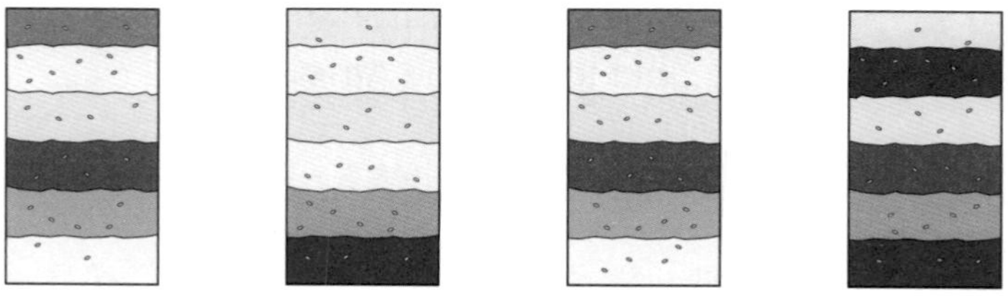

Continent A   **Continent B**   **Continent C**   **Continent D**

   a)   Which two continents do you think were joined at one time? Explain your answer.

....

....

   b)   Suggest what other piece of evidence in the rock formation may back this up.

....

....

Evidence for Plate Tectonics

Q4 Wegener studied astronomy at Berlin University in 1904. His fascination with observing identical fossils on both sides of the Atlantic led him to produce his theory of continental drift in 1915.

Tick the correct boxes to show whether the following statements are **true** or **false**.

		True	False
a)	Wegener found that each continent had its own unrelated collection of plant and animal fossils.	☐	☐
b)	The Earth's continents seem to fit together like a big jigsaw.	☐	☐
c)	Rock formations are made of layers, which are different on every continent.	☐	☐
d)	Wegener studied fossils on both sides of the Pacific Ocean.	☐	☐
e)	Wegener had a PhD in geology.	☐	☐
f)	Investigations of the ocean floor showed that although Wegener wasn't absolutely right, his ideas were pretty close.	☐	☐
g)	Wegener's theory was **not** readily accepted by scientists at the time.	☐	☐

Q5 Wegener's theory of continental drift was put forward after he found **evidence**. List four pieces of evidence that Wegener found.

1. ....
....

2. ....
....

3. ....
....

4. ....
....
....

Top Tips: It was pretty impressive how Wegener came up with his fairly accurate theory based on the available clues. But it's a pity that it took so long to find more evidence for Wegener's theory — I bet he would have really enjoyed looking smug and telling everyone, "I told you so."

Volcanic Eruptions

Q1   Answer the following questions.

  a)   What is the difference between magma and lava?

....

  b)   How is igneous rock formed?

....

  c)   The type of igneous rock formed depends on two things. What are they?

....

Q2   Number these processes in the correct order to explain **how volcanoes may form**.

☐   Molten rock forces its way to the surface, forming a volcano.

☐   The denser oceanic crust is forced underground (subduction).

☐   Continental crust and oceanic crust collide.

☐   Rock melts underground, forming magma.

Q3   The diagram shows the formation of a volcano at the boundary
           between an oceanic plate and a continental plate.

  a)   **Label the diagram** using the words in the box.

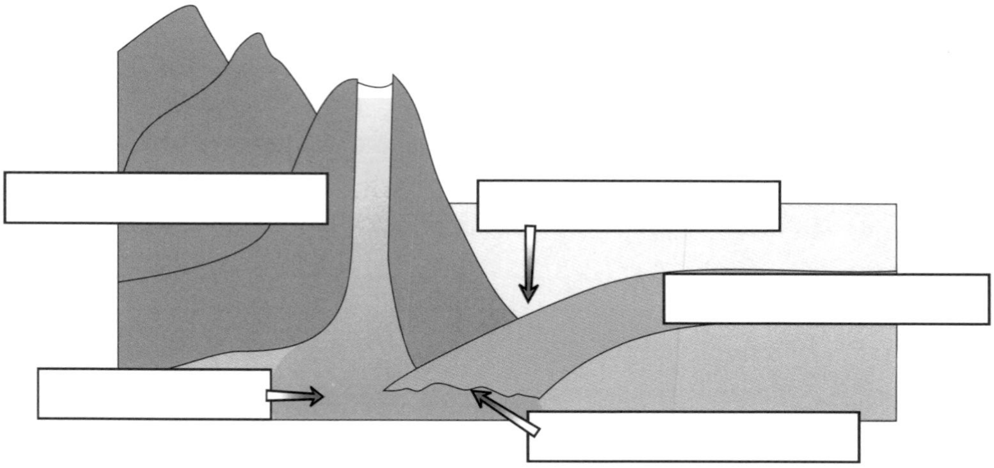

| oceanic trench |
| melting |
| oceanic plate |
| continental plate |
| magma |

  b)   This type of plate boundary is called a "**subduction zone**". What is meant by subduction?

....

  c)   What happens to the oceanic plate as it is forced down under the continental plate?

....

Volcanic Eruptions

Q4   Off the coast of Chile, the oceanic Nazca plate is being forced **under** the South American plate.

Explain how this accounts for the following:

a)   The region has many volcanoes.

....

....

b)   The region also has many earthquakes.

....

c)   Where the plates meet, the sea is very deep.

....

....

d)   There is a huge mountain range along the edge of the continental plate.

....

....

Q5   Imagine you live near an active volcano. This volcano only produces **iron-rich basalt** magma.

a)   Explain why living here is relatively safe.

....

b)   Why would it be much more dangerous living near a volcano that produces **silica-rich rhyolite**?

....

....

c)   Explain why some people live near volcanoes, even though there are dangers.

....

....

d)   Sometimes volcanic material forms graded beds. Explain what this means.

....

....

....

The Evolution of the Atmosphere

Q1   Tick the boxes next to the sentences below that are **true**.

When the Earth was formed, its surface was molten. ☐

The Earth's early atmosphere is thought to have been mostly oxygen. ☐

When oxygen started building up in the atmosphere, all organisms began to thrive. ☐

When some plants died and were buried under layers of sediment, the carbon
they had removed from the atmosphere became locked up as fossil fuels. ☐

The development of the ozone layer meant that the Earth's temperature
became suitable for complex organisms like us to evolve. ☐

Q2   The amount of **carbon dioxide** in the atmosphere has changed over the last 4.5 billion or so years.

Describe how the level of carbon dioxide has changed and explain why this change happened.

....

....

....

....

Q3   Draw lines to put the statements in the **right order** on the timeline. One has been done for you.

Present

NOT TO
SCALE

4600 million years ago

The Earth cooled down slightly.
A thin crust formed.

Water vapour condensed to form oceans.

The Earth formed.
There was lots of volcanic activity.

More complex organisms evolved.

Plant life appeared.

The atmosphere is about four-fifths
nitrogen and one-fifth oxygen.

Oxygen built up due to photosynthesis,
and the ozone layer developed.

Don't get confused — 4600 million
is the same as 4.6 billion.

Module C2 — Rocks and Metals

The Evolution of the Atmosphere

Q4 The pie chart below shows the proportions of different gases in the Earth's atmosphere today.

a) Add the labels '**Nitrogen**', '**Oxygen**', and '**Carbon dioxide and other gases**'.

b) Give the approximate percentages of the following gases in the air today:

Nitrogen ....

Oxygen ....

Carbon dioxide ....

Earth's Atmosphere Today

c) This pie chart shows the proportions of different gases that we think were in the Earth's atmosphere 4500 million years ago.

Earth's Atmosphere 4500 Million Years Ago

Carbon dioxide

Ammonia

Other gases

Water vapour

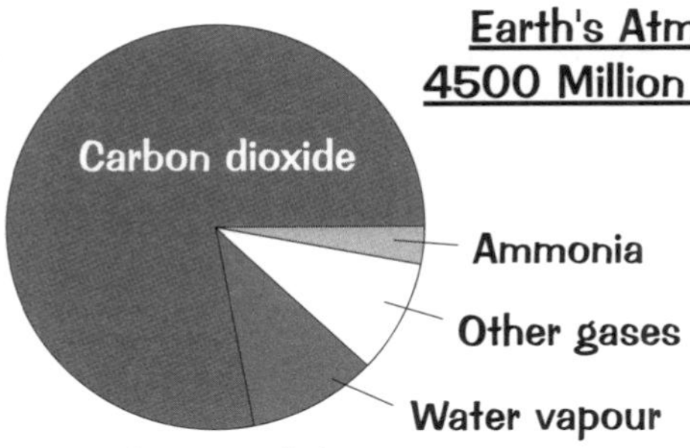

Describe the main differences between today's atmosphere and the atmosphere 4500 million years ago.

....

....

d) Explain why the amount of water vapour has decreased.

....

What did the water vapour change into?

....

e) Explain how oxygen was introduced into the atmosphere.

....

f) Give two effects of the oxygen levels in the atmosphere rising.

1. ....

....

2. ....

....

g) Give two ways that nitrogen was added to the atmosphere.

1. ....

2. ....

The Carbon Cycle

Q1   Here is a diagram of the **carbon cycle**.

a)   What is process A? ....

b)   What is process B? ....

c)   Process C could be decay. What else could it be?

....

d)   What is substance D? ....

Q2   Carbon that was once part of Henry VIII could now be part of you.

Name each process in the diagram.

A ....

B ....

C ....

D ....

Q3   The **human population** is increasing rapidly and this increase is affecting the atmosphere.

List **three** reasons why this dramatic increase in population has caused a rise in CO_2 levels.

....

....

....

Sid's day

8.00 am: Wakes up, fills the kettle to the top and makes a cup of tea to enjoy with his pineapple, which was harvested in Guatemala.

10.00 am: Drives to the travel agent in his shiny new 4X4 car and books a holiday in Hawaii departing that evening.

11.00 am: Goes shopping for a grass skirt.

11.30 am: Returns home and decides to put on his grass skirt. But it's a bit chilly, so he puts the heating on high.

5.00 pm: Departs for the airport, leaving all the lights and the TV on to keep burglars away.

Q4   On the left is some information about what Sid does one day.

Suggest three ways that Sid could have lowered the amount of carbon dioxide he produced.

....

....

....

Top Tips: It's tough minimising your carbon emissions when you live in a world of cheap flights, abundant plastic bags, supermarkets filled with cheap exotic food, and central heating. But if we carry on the way we're going, the world's likely to be in a lot of trouble one day.

Module C2 — Rocks and Metals

Air Pollution and Acid Rain

Q1   Use the words and phrases below to complete the paragraph.

| nitric | sulfur dioxide | the greenhouse effect | sulfuric | nitrogen oxides | acid rain |

When fossil fuels are burned carbon dioxide is produced. The main problem caused by

this is .... The gas .... is also

produced. This comes from sulfur impurities in the fuel. When it combines with

moisture in the air .... acid is produced. This falls as acid rain.

In the high temperatures inside a car engine nitrogen and oxygen from the air react

together to produce .... These react with moisture to produce

.... acid, which is another cause of acid rain.

Q2   **Acid rain** causes a variety of problems.

a)   Why might architects choose **not** to build from limestone in polluted cities?

....

b)   Give **two** other consequences of acid rain.

....

c)   What steps are taken to try to avoid **power stations** contributing to acid rain?

....

Q3   **Ozone** causes problems when it forms at **ground level**.

a)   What are these problems? ....

b)   **Underline** the things below which are normally involved in the formation of **ground-level ozone**.

nitrogen   oxygen   carbon dioxide   sunlight   oxides of nitrogen   sulfur dioxide

Q4   **Exhaust fumes** from cars and lorries often contain **carbon monoxide**.

a)   Why is carbon monoxide more likely to be formed in engines than if fuel is burnt in the open air?

....

b)   Why is carbon monoxide so dangerous?

....

Q5   **Catalytic converters** reduce the amount of harmful gases that are released into the atmosphere.

a)   Complete the following equations to show a reaction that occurs in a catalytic converter:

i)   carbon monoxide + nitrogen oxide → .... + ...

ii)   ....CO + ...NO → .... + ...

b)   What catalyst is usually used for this reaction? ....

Module C2 — Rocks and Metals

Chemical Reaction Rates

Q1   Match these common chemical reactions to the **speed** at which they happen.

a firework exploding

SLOW (hours or longer)

a match burning

hair being dyed

MODERATE SPEED (minutes)

an apple rotting

FAST (seconds or shorter)

oil paint drying

Q2   Indicate whether the following statements are **true** or **false**.

                                                                               True False

a)   Reaction rates depend on the temperature.

b)   When particles collide they always react.

c)   A catalyst can change the rate of a reaction.

d)   Collision theory helps us to explain rates of reaction.

Q3   The rate of the reaction below can be followed by measuring the change in mass.

$$CaCO_3 + 2HCl \rightarrow CaCl_2 + CO_2 + H_2O$$

a)   Explain why the rate of this reaction can be followed in this way.

....

Think about the states of the products.

b)   Describe another way in which this reaction could be followed.
Draw a diagram in the space on the right to illustrate your answer.

....

....

....

c)   Why could you not follow the reaction below by measuring the change in mass?

$$H_2SO_4 + 2NaOH \rightarrow Na_2SO_4 + 2H_2O$$

....

....

Q4   **Collision theory** explains reaction rates perfectly.

Give two factors that determine whether or not two particles will react.

....

....

Top Tips: Remember — there'll only be a change of mass in a reaction if a product is **lost** from the beaker or whatever you're weighing. This'll be a **gas** that wafts away into the surroundings.

Collision Theory

Q1 Draw lines to match up the changes with their effects on the particles.

increasing the temperature

decreasing the concentration

adding a catalyst

increasing the surface area

provides a surface for particles to stick to and lowers activation energy

makes the particles move faster, so they collide more often

means more of a solid reactant will be exposed to the other reactant

means fewer particles of reactants are present, so fewer collisions occur

Q2 Reactions involving gases are affected by the **pressure**.

a) i) If you increase the pressure of a gas reaction, does the rate **increase** or **decrease**? ....

ii) Explain your answer.

....

....

b) In the boxes on the right, draw two diagrams, one showing particles of two different gases at low pressure, the other showing the gases at high pressure.

low pressure   **high pressure**

Q3 Here are five statements about **surface area** and rates of reaction. Tick the appropriate box to show whether each is true or false.

True   False

a) Breaking a solid into smaller pieces decreases its surface area. ☐ ☐

b) A larger surface area will mean a faster rate of reaction. ☐ ☐

c) A larger surface area decreases the number of useful collisions. ☐ ☐

d) Powdered marble has a larger surface area than the same mass of marble chips. ☐ ☐

e) A powdered solid reactant produces more product overall than an equal mass of reactant in large lumps does. ☐ ☐

Q4 **Catalysts** affect particle collisions in a different way from changes in concentration and surface area.

a) Explain how a catalyst works.

....

....

b) Do catalysts **increase** or **decrease** the number of **successful** collisions? ....

Collision Theory

Q5 Use some of the words below to complete the paragraph.

| successful | slowing down | slower | surface area | speeding up |
| faster | energy | increases | decreases | unsuccessful |

When a reacting mixture is heated, the particles move ....

This .... the number of collisions. It also gives the particles

more .... so more collisions are ....

All this leads to the reaction ....

Q6 Which of the following statements are **true** and which are **false**?

True False

a) Adding a catalyst will produce more products. ☐ ☐

b) A reaction is usually fastest at the beginning. ☐ ☐

c) The gradient of a reaction rate graph tells you the rate at that point. ☐ ☐

d) You cannot tell from a reaction rate graph when the reaction has stopped. ☐ ☐

e) You would expect a piece of magnesium to disappear faster when
placed in concentrated acid than when placed in dilute acid. ☐ ☐

Q7 Matilda conducted an experiment to investigate the effect of **surface area** on the rate of reaction.
She added excess dilute hydrochloric acid to **large marble chips** and measured the loss of mass
at regular time intervals. She repeated the experiment using the same mass of **powdered marble**.
Below is a graph of her results.

a) Which curve, A or B, was
obtained when **large pieces**
of marble were used? ....

b) On the graph opposite, draw:

i) the curve you would expect if you
used the **same mass** of **medium**
sized marble pieces. Label it C.

ii) the curve you would expect if you
used **half** the mass of medium
sized marble pieces. Label it D.

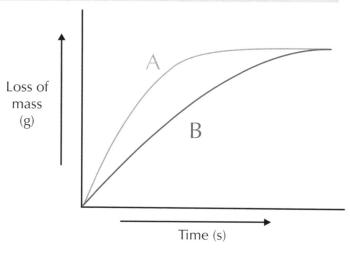

c) Name the **independent** variable in this investigation. ....

d) Is there enough information given above for you to be sure whether this was a **fair test** or not?
Explain your answer.

....

....

Collision Theory

Q8 The data below shows how much **carbon dioxide** was given off during the reaction of 5 g of **marble chips** (calcium carbonate) with 100 cm³ of hydrochloric acid.

a) On the grid below, plot a graph of **volume of carbon dioxide** (vertical axis) against **time** (horizontal axis) for **reaction 1**. Label it.

b) On the same axis, plot a similar graph for **reaction 2**. Label it.

	REACTION 1	REACTION 2
Time (s)	Volume of CO_2 produced (cm³)	Volume of CO_2 produced (cm³)
10	14	24
20	25	42
30	36	57
40	46	69
50	54	77
60	62	80
70	70	80
80	76	80
90	80	80
100	80	80

c) Which reaction is faster? Explain how you know this.

....

d) Suggest **three** possible causes of the difference in **rate** between reaction 1 and reaction 2.

....

....

....

e) On your graph label where: **i)** reaction 2 **finished**.   **ii)** reaction 2 had its **fastest rate**.

f) Calculate the rate of reaction for both reaction 1 and reaction 2 at 20 s.

....

....

g) Does this back up your answer to **c**? ....

h) What volume of carbon dioxide had been produced in **reaction 1** after **25 seconds**? ....

Read the value off the graph you have drawn.

Q9 The sign on the right is displayed on the doors of a custard factory. Other than hygiene, explain why these rules are important.

DANGER
NO SMOKING, MATCHES OR OPEN LIGHTS

....

....

Mixed Questions — Module C2

Q1   **Limestone** is a sedimentary rock.

a)   Describe the main steps in the formation of sedimentary rocks.

....

....

....

b)   Complete the following equation to show the **thermal decomposition** of limestone.

$$CaCO_3 \rightarrow \text{............} + \text{............}$$

c)   Limestone can be processed to form useful building materials. Complete the flow diagram.

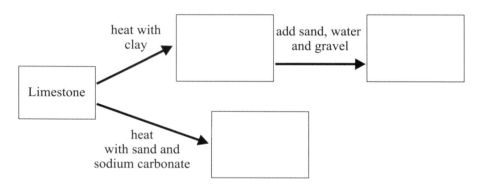

Q2   Dillon was investigating how different **concentrations** of acid affect the rate of a reaction.

a)   The diagram shows the acid particles present in a solution of dilute acid.

Draw a similar diagram with the same volume of liquid but at a **higher concentration**.

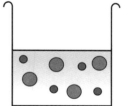 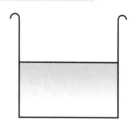

b)   Explain how increasing the concentration of the acid will affect the reaction rate.

....

....

c)   On these axes, draw and label sketches of the curves you would expect for a **high** and a **low** concentration of acid. (Assume that the acid is not the limiting reactant.)

d)   Name two things Dillon will need to keep constant in order to make it a fair experiment.

1. ....

2. ....

Mixed Questions — Module C2

Q3 Copper is a metal with a variety of uses.

a) Copper is dug out of the ground as an **ore**. Explain what an **ore** is.

....

b) Copper is used in **alloys**. Circle the alloys below which contain copper.

   bronze   amalgam   brass   steel   solder   nitinol

c) The diagram below shows how copper is purified. Label the **anode** and the **cathode**.

d) What makes copper atoms go into solution as ions?

....

....

e) Which electrode increases in size during the electrolysis?

....

f) What is purified copper used for in cars? Why is this?

....

g) Name another **metal element** which is used in cars. What part of the car is it used for and why?

....

....

h) Explain how **recycling** the copper and other metals used in cars could help slow the rise in atmospheric carbon dioxide levels.

....

....

Q4 A **subduction zone** occurs where an oceanic plate and a continental plate collide.

a) What happens to the plates at a subduction zone?

....

b) Explain how the following are formed at a subduction zone:

   i) magma ....

   ....

   ii) mountains ....

   ....

c) What sea-floor feature is formed at a subduction zone? ....

Module C2 — Rocks and Metals

Mixed Questions — Module C2

Q5 The diagram shows some details of the 'rock cycle'.

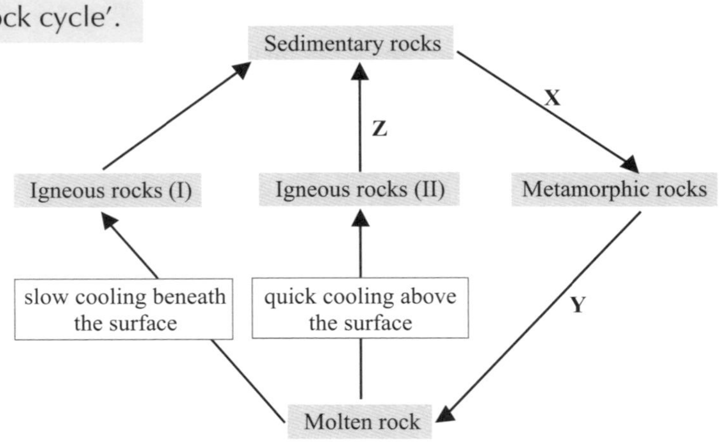

a) Name an igneous rock of type I.

....

b) Name an igneous rock of type II.

....

c) What physical change takes place in the process labelled Y on the diagram?

....

d) Which two physical conditions bring about the change labelled X on the diagram above?

....

Diagram labels:
Sedimentary rocks
Igneous rocks (I)   Igneous rocks (II)   Metamorphic rocks
X   Z   Y
slow cooling beneath the surface   quick cooling above the surface
Molten rock

Q6 The atmosphere of Mars consists of 95.3% carbon dioxide, 2.7% nitrogen, and 2% of other gases.

a) Describe the similarities between this and the early atmosphere of Earth.

....

....

b) Describe the differences between the compositions of the atmospheres of Mars and Earth today.

....

....

c) Describe how human activity is affecting the composition of the air.

....

....

Q7 Lucas decides to raffle off an extra large **garden gnome** which he has made.

a) He's concerned that some people may forge raffle tickets to get their hands on the prize. Describe how **special pigments** could be used to thwart the forgers.

....

....

b) Lucas used oil paints on his gnome. Why did this paint take longer to dry than emulsion would?

....

Atoms

Q1 **Complete** the following sentences.

a) Neutral atoms have a charge of ....

b) A charged atom is called an ....

c) A neutral atom has the same number of .... and ....

d) If an electron is added to a neutral atom, the atom becomes .... charged.

Q2 **Complete** this table.

Particle	Mass	Charge
Proton	1	
	1	0
Electron		−1

Q3 **What am I?**

Choose from: **nucleus**   **proton**   **electron**   **neutron**

a) I am in the centre of the atom. I contain protons and neutrons. ....

b) I move around the nucleus in a shell. ....

c) I am the lightest. ....

d) I am positively charged. ....

e) I am relatively heavy and have no charge. ....

f) In a neutral atom there are as many of me as there are electrons. ....

Q4 Elements have a **mass number** and an **atomic number**.

a) What does the **mass number** of an element tell you?

....

b) What does the **atomic number** of an element tell you?

....

c) Fill in this table using a periodic table.

Element	Symbol	Mass Number	Number of Protons	Number of Electrons	Number of Neutrons
Sodium	Na		11		
		16	8	8	8
Neon			10	10	10
	Ca			20	20

Isotopes, Elements and Compounds

Q1 a) Correctly label the following diagrams with either '**element**' or '**compound**'.

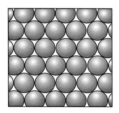   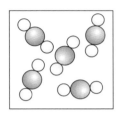   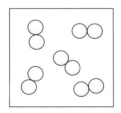   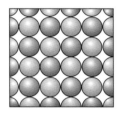

A = ...   B = ...   C = ...   D= ....

b) Suggest which diagram (A, B, C or D) could represent:

i) oxygen ....   **ii)** sodium ....   **iii)** sodium chloride ....   **iv)** carbon dioxide ....

Q2 Circle the **correct words** in these sentences.

a) **Compounds / Atoms** are formed when two or more elements react together.

b) The properties of compounds are **exactly the same as / completely different to** those of the original elements.

c) It is **easy / difficult** to separate the elements in a compound.

d) Carbon dioxide is **a compound / an element**, whereas iron is **a compound / an element**.

e) The number of **neutrons / electrons** determines the chemistry of an element.

Q3 Choose the correct words to **complete** this paragraph.

element	isotopes	protons	neutrons

.... are different atomic forms of the same .... which have the same number of .... but a different number of ....

Q4 Which of the following atoms are **isotopes** of each other? Explain your answer.

W $^{12}_{6}C$ **X** $^{4}_{2}He$ **Y** $^{14}_{6}C$ **Z** $^{14}_{7}N$

Answer: .... and ....

Explanation: ....

Q5 Describe the following types of **chemical bonding**:

a) Ionic ....

b) Covalent ....

The Periodic Table

Q1 Select from these **elements** to answer the following questions.

iodine   nickel   silicon   sodium   radon   krypton   calcium

a) Which two elements are in the same group? .... and ....

b) Name two elements which are in Period 3. .... and ....

c) Name an alkali metal. ....

d) Name a transition metal. ....

e) Name an element with seven electrons in its outer shell. ....

f) Name a non-metal which is not in Group 8. ....

Q2 Tick the correct boxes to show whether these statements are **true** or **false**.   True False

a) Elements in the same **group** have the same number of electrons in their outer shell. ☐ ☐

b) The periodic table shows the elements in order of ascending **atomic mass**. ☐ ☐

c) Each **column** in the periodic table contains elements with similar properties. ☐ ☐

d) The periodic table is made up of all the known compounds. ☐ ☐

e) There are more than 100 known elements. ☐ ☐

f) Each new period in the periodic table represents another full shell of electrons. ☐ ☐

Q3 Elements in the same group undergo **similar reactions**.

a) Tick the pairs of elements that would undergo similar reactions.

A potassium and rubidium ☐   **C** calcium and oxygen ☐

B helium and fluorine ☐   **D** nitrogen and arsenic ☐

b) Explain why fluorine and chlorine undergo similar reactions.

....

....

Q4 Complete the following table.

	Alternative Name	Number of Electrons in Outer Shell
Group 1		
Group 7		
Group 8		*

* excluding helium

Electron Shells

Q1 a) Tick the boxes to show whether the statements are **true** or **false**. **True False**

    i) Electrons occupy shells.

    ii) The highest energy levels are always filled first.

    iii) Atoms are most stable when they have partially filled shells.

    iv) Noble gases have a full outer shell of electrons.

    v) Reactive elements have full outer shells.

b) Write out corrected versions of the **false** statements.

....

....

....

Q2 Identify **two** things that are wrong with this diagram.

1. ....

....

2. ....

....

Q3 Write out the **electronic configuration** for each of the following elements.

a) Beryllium .... **d)** Calcium ....

b) Oxygen .... **e)** Aluminium ....

c) Silicon .... **f)** Argon ....

Q4 Do the following groups contain **reactive** or **unreactive** elements? Explain your answers in terms of **electron shells**.

a) Noble gases (Group 8) ....

....

b) Alkali metals (Group 1) ....

....

Electron Shells

Q5   **Chlorine** has an atomic number of 17.

a)   What is chlorine's electron configuration? ....

b)   Draw the electrons on the shells in the diagram.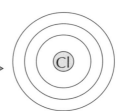

c)   Why does chlorine react readily?

....

Q6   Draw the **full electronic arrangements** for these elements. (The first three have been done for you.)

Hydrogen   Helium   Lithium

a) Carbon   **b)** Nitrogen   **c)** Fluorine

   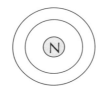   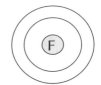

d) Sodium   **e)** Magnesium   **f)** Phosphorus

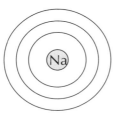   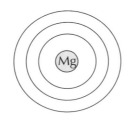   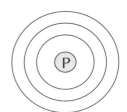

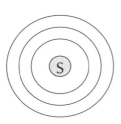   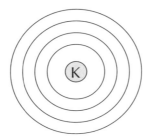   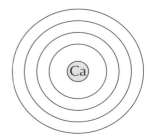

g) Sulfur   **h)** Potassium   **i)** Calcium

Top Tips: Once you've learnt the 'electron shell rules' these are pretty easy — the first shell can only take 2 electrons, and the second and third shells a maximum of 8 each. Don't forget it.

Ionic Bonding

Q1 Fill in the gaps in the sentences below by choosing the correct words from the box.

> protons   charged particles   repelled by
>
> electrons   ions   attracted to   neutral particles

a) In ionic bonding atoms lose or gain .... to form ....

b) Ions are ....

c) Ions with opposite charges are strongly .... each other.

Q2 Tick the correct boxes to show whether the following statements are **true** or **false**.

		True	False
a)	Metals have low numbers of electrons in their outer shells.	☐	☐
b)	Metals form negatively charged ions.	☐	☐
c)	Elements in Group 7 gain electrons when they react.	☐	☐
d)	Atoms form ions because they are more stable when they have full outer shells.	☐	☐
e)	Elements in Group 8 are very reactive.	☐	☐

Q3 Use this **diagram** to answer the following questions.

a) Which **group** of the periodic table does **sodium** belong to? ....

b) How many **electrons** does **chlorine** need to gain to get a full outer shell of electrons? ....

c) What is the **charge** on a **sodium ion**? ....

d) What is the chemical formula of **sodium chloride**? ....

Q4 Here are some elements and the ions they form:

beryllium, Be^{2+} potassium, K^+ iodine, I^- sulfur, S^{2-}

Make sure the charges on the ions balance.

Write down the formulas of four compounds which can be made using these elements.

1. ....   2. ....

3. ....   4. ....

Ions and Ionic Compounds

Q1 Magnesium and oxygen react to form **magnesium oxide**, an **ionic** compound.

a) Draw a 'dot and cross' diagram showing the formation of magnesium oxide from magnesium and oxygen atoms.

b) What name is given to the structure of magnesium oxide?

....

c) Circle the correct words to explain why magnesium oxide has a high melting point.

> Magnesium oxide has very **strong** / **weak** chemical bonds between the **negative** / **positive** magnesium ions and the **negative** / **positive** oxygen ions. This means that it takes a **small** / **large** amount of energy to break the bonds and melt the compound.

Q2 Mike conducts an experiment to find out if **sodium chloride** conducts electricity. He tests the compound when it's solid, when it's dissolved in water and when it's molten.

	Conducts electricity?
When solid	
When dissolved in water	
When molten	

a) Complete the table of results opposite.

b) Explain your answers to part a).

....

....

....

Q3 Draw '**dot and cross**' diagrams showing the formation of the following ionic compounds:

a) sodium oxide

b) magnesium chloride

Module C3 — The Periodic Table

Group 1 — Alkali Metals

Q1   Indicate whether the statements below are **true** or **false**.

	True	False

a)   Alkali metals readily gain electrons to form 1^+ ions.   ☐ ☐

b)   Alkali metals form covalent compounds by sharing electrons.   ☐ ☐

c)   Alkali metals are stored in oil to stop them reacting with oxygen and water in the air.   ☐ ☐

d)   Alkali metal atoms all have a single electron in their outer shell.   ☐ ☐

e)   Alkali metals are hard.   ☐ ☐

Q2   The table shows the **melting points** of some Group 1 metals.

Element	Melting point (°C)
Li	181
Na	98
K	63
Rb	39
Cs	?

a)   What is unusual about the **melting points** of the alkali metals compared to other metals?

....

b)   Would you expect the melting point of **caesium** to be higher or lower than **rubidium**? Explain your answer.

....

c)   Complete the following sentence:

As you move down Group 1, the reactivity of the atoms ....**.**

Q3   Archibald put a piece of **lithium** into a beaker of water.

a)   Explain why the lithium floated on top of the water.

....

b)   After the reaction had finished, Archibald tested the water with universal indicator. What colour change would he see, and why?

....

....

c)   Write a **balanced symbol equation** for the reaction.

....

d)   **i)**   Write a word equation for the reaction between rubidium and water.

....

ii)   Would you expect the reaction between rubidium and water to be **more** or **less** vigorous than the reaction between lithium and water? Explain your answer.

....

Archibald

"squeaky pop!"

Group 1 — Alkali Metals

Q4   Alkali metal compounds emit characteristic **colours** when heated.

a)   Selina has three powdered samples of alkali metal compounds. Describe an experiment she could carry out to help her identify the alkali metal present.

....

....

....

....

b)   Which **alkali metal** is present in:

i)   an alkali metal nitrate (found in gunpowder) that burns with a lilac flame? ....

ii)   a street lamp that emits an orange light? ....

iii)   fireworks that produce red flames? ....

Q5   Sodium and potassium are **alkali metals**.

a)   Draw the electronic arrangements of a **sodium atom** and a **potassium atom** in the space provided.

b)   i)   Write a balanced symbol equation to show the formation of a sodium ion from a sodium atom.

....

ii)   Is this process oxidation or reduction? Explain your answer.

....

c)   Why do sodium and potassium have similar properties?

....

d)   Why is potassium more reactive than sodium?

....

....

Top Tip: All the alkali metals have a single outer electron, which they're dead keen to get rid of so they have a nice full outer shell. As you move down the group the outer electron gets further away from the nucleus so it's lost more easily — this makes the elements more reactive as you go down the group.

Electrolysis and the Half-Equations

Q1 Draw lines to join the words with their correct meanings.

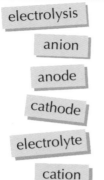

electrolysis — the positive electrode

anion — the breakdown of a substance using electricity

anode — positive ion that is attracted to the cathode

cathode — negative ion that is attracted to the anode

electrolyte — the negative electrode

cation — the liquid that is used in electrolysis

Q2 Explain why the electrolyte needs to be either a **solution** or **molten** for electrolysis to work.

....

....

Q3 The diagram below shows the electrolysis of **sulfuric acid solution**.

a) Identify the ions and molecules labelled A, B, C and D on the diagram.

Choose from the options in the box below.

O^{2-} H^+ O_2 H_2
OH^- H_2SO_4 H_2O

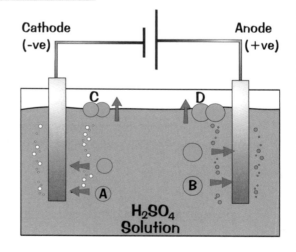

A ....   B ....

C ....   D ....

b) Write **balanced** half-equations for the processes that occur during the electrolysis of sulfuric acid solution.

Make sure the charges balance.

Cathode: ....

Anode: ....

c) Why can't pure water be electrolysed?

....

Top Tips: Half-equations just show what's going on at the cathode and anode in terms of electrons — a positive ion gains electrons and a negative ion loses electrons.

Extracting Aluminium

Q1   **Aluminium** is the most **abundant** metal in the Earth's crust.

Goodness, how awfully common... ₒ°°ₒ

a)   **i)**   Circle the correct word:

The most common aluminium ore is bauxite / cryolite.

ii)   When this ore is mined and purified, which compound is obtained? Give its name and formula.

Name ....   **Formula** ....

b)   Why can't aluminium be extracted by **reduction** with carbon?

....

c)   Although it's very common, aluminium was not discovered until 1825. Suggest why.

....

Q2 a)   Indicate whether the following statements are **true** or **false**.

True   False

i)   Ionic substances can only be electrolysed if molten or in solution.   ☐ ☐

ii)   In the extraction of aluminium the electrolyte is molten aluminium metal.   ☐ ☐

iii)   Aluminium oxide is dissolved in molten cryolite before electrolysis begins.   ☐ ☐

iv)   Copper electrodes are used in the extraction of aluminium by electrolysis.   ☐ ☐

v)   Aluminium is formed at the anode.   ☐ ☐

b)   Write out a correct version of each false statement.

....

....

....

....

Q3   The extraction of aluminium by electrolysis is a **redox reaction**.

a)   Write balanced half-equations for the reactions at the electrodes.

Cathode: ....

Anode: ....

b)   Use the half-equations to help explain why this process is called a 'redox' reaction.

....

....

Extracting Aluminium

Q4 The diagram shows the set-up of the equipment used to **extract** aluminium by **electrolysis**.

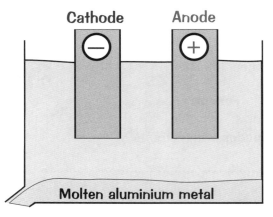

Cathode   Anode

Molten aluminium metal

Vote ROLYSIS —
Keep our
Aluminium
Industry
working!

Rolysis
for
President!

a) Why is the aluminium formed as a **liquid**?

....

b) What substance is formed at the anode? ....

c) Why does the anode need to be replaced frequently?

....

....

Q5 **Bauxite**, mined in Jamaica, is shipped to Canada to be processed into aluminium because Canada has abundant **hydroelectric power**.

a) Give three major costs, apart from the mining of the ore, involved in the extraction of aluminium.

1. ....

2. ....

3. ....

b) Why does it make economic sense to ship the ore to Canada?

....

....

Top Tips: In general, things that are **common** and **easy to get at** are **cheap**. Like potatoes, say. But you can't make drink cans or aeroplane fuselages from potatoes — you need a nice **lightweight metal**, like aluminium. Aluminium is as common a metal as you can get but it's not that cheap because it's expensive to extract — electrolysis costs a lot. (Potatoes, on the other hand, are very easy to extract — you find a **spade** and just get **digging** — no pricey electricity needed.)

Module C3 — The Periodic Table

Covalent Bonding

Q1 Indicate whether each statement is **true** or **false**.

True False

a) Covalent bonding involves sharing electrons.

b) Atoms react to gain a full outer shell of electrons.

c) Some atoms can make both ionic and covalent bonds.

d) Hydrogen can form two covalent bonds.

e) Carbon can form four covalent bonds.

"Oi, give me that electron big nose!"

Q2 Complete these sentences by circling the correct word from each pair.

a) Substances that contain covalent bonds usually have **giant / simple** molecular structures.

b) Atoms within covalent molecules are held together by **strong / weak** covalent bonds.

c) Intermolecular forces in covalent substances are **strong / weak**. This results in **high / low** melting and boiling points.

d) Molecular substances **do / don't** conduct electricity.

Q3 Complete the following diagrams by adding **electrons**. Only the **outer shells** are shown.

Use • and x to show the electrons from the different elements.

a) Hydrogen (H_2)

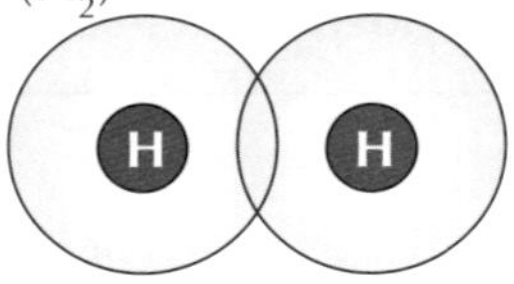

d) Water (H_2O)

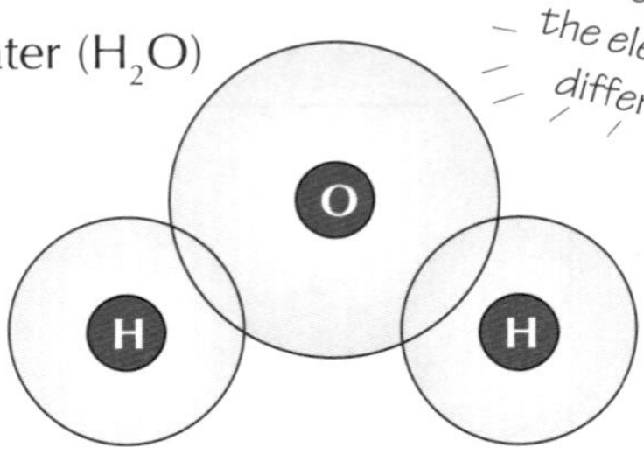

b) Chlorine (Cl_2)

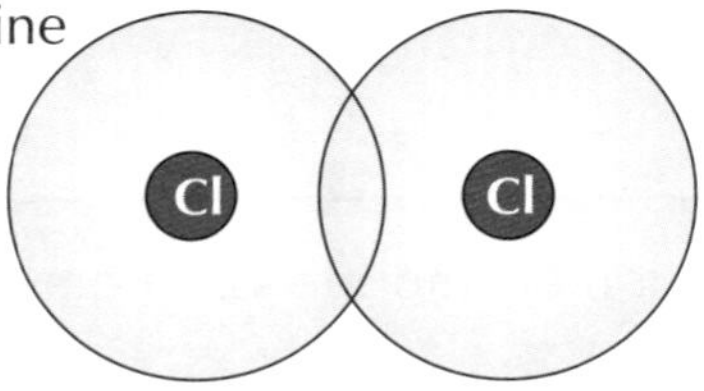

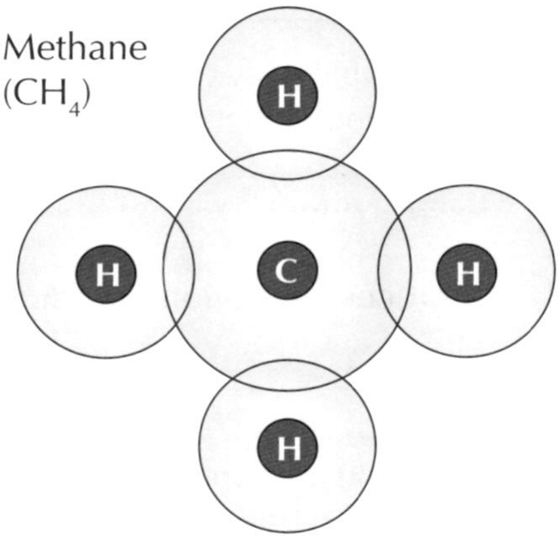

c) Carbon dioxide (CO_2)

e) Methane (CH_4)

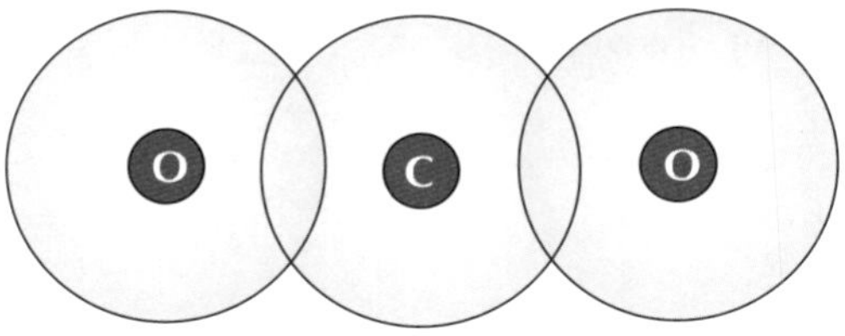

Q4 Explain why chlorine exists as Cl_2 molecules, and not as single atoms.

....

....

Group 7 — Halogens

Q1   Draw lines to match each halogen to its **description**.

chlorine

iodine

bromine

dense green gas

orange liquid

dark grey solid

Hubba hubba

Q2   Tick the correct boxes to say whether these statements are **true** or **false**.

		True	False
a)	Chlorine gas is made up of molecules which each contain three chlorine atoms.	☐	☐
b)	Halogens covalently bond with other non-metals to form molecules.	☐	☐
c)	Chlorine reacts with hydrogen to form an ionic compound.	☐	☐
d)	The halogens become less reactive as you go down the group.	☐	☐
e)	Chlorine and bromine are poisonous.	☐	☐
f)	The halogens readily gain electrons to form 1^+ ions.	☐	☐

Q3   Chlorine and bromine are both **halogens**.

a)   Draw the electron arrangements of a **chlorine atom** and a **chloride ion** in the space provided.

b) i)   Write a balanced symbol equation to show the formation of chloride ions from a chlorine molecule.

....

ii)   Is this process oxidation or reduction? Explain your answer.

....

c)   Why do chlorine and bromine have similar properties?

....

d)   Why is bromine less reactive than chlorine?

....

Group 7 — Halogens

Q4 **Sodium** was reacted with **bromine vapour** using the equipment shown. White crystals of a new solid were formed during the reaction.

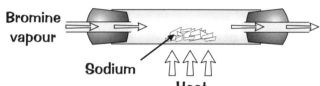

Bromine vapour

Sodium

Heat

a) Name the white crystals.

....

b) Write a balanced symbol equation for the reaction.

....

c) Would you expect the above reaction to be faster or slower than a similar reaction between:

i) sodium and iodine vapour? Explain your answer.

....

ii) sodium and chlorine vapour? Explain your answer.

....

Q5 Equal volumes of **bromine water** were added to two test tubes, each containing a different **potassium halide solution**. The results are shown in the table.

SOLUTION	RESULT
potassium chloride	no colour change
potassium iodide	colour change

a) Explain these results.

....

....

....

b) Write a **balanced symbol equation** for the reaction in the potassium iodide solution.

....

c) Would you expect a reaction between:

i) bromine water and potassium astatide? ....

ii) bromine water and potassium fluoride? ....

Module C3 — The Periodic Table

Metals

Q1 Draw a diagram in the space below to show the arrangement of the atoms in a typical **metal**. Label the **atoms** and the **free electrons**, and show any relevant charges.

Q2 The table shows the properties of **four elements** found in the periodic table.

ELEMENT	MELTING POINT (°C)	DENSITY (g/cm³)	ELECTRICAL CONDUCTIVITY
A	1084	8.9	Excellent
B	–39	13.6	Very good
C	3500	3.51	Very poor
D	1536	7.87	Very good

a) Which three of the above elements are most likely to be **metals**?

....

b) Explain how you know the other element is **not** a metal.

....

....

c) Suggest the name of **element B** and explain your answer.

....

....

Q3 Explain how **electricity** is conducted through metals.

....

....

Metals

Q4 Complete the following sentences by choosing from the words in the box.

Each word should only be used once.

hammered	weak	low	high	strong	malleable	folded

a) Metals have a .... tensile strength.

b) Metals are .... and hard to break.

c) Metals can be .... into different shapes because they are ....

Q5 Explain why most metals have **high melting points**.

....

....

Q6 **Metals** are used for different things depending on their **properties**.

For each of the uses below, choose the most suitable metal from the list and state one property of the metal that makes it suitable for this purpose.

stainless steel   copper   aluminium   steel

a) Structures like bridges.

Metal ....

Property ....

b) Aeroplanes.

Metal ....

Property ....

c) Cutlery.

Metal ....

Property ....

d) Electrical wiring.

Metal ....

Property ....

Top Tip: Okay, so metals form weird bonds. How come the electrons can go wandering about like that? Well actually, that's just the kind of question you **don't** need to ask yourself right now. Don't stress about it, just learn the key phrases examiners like — '**giant structure**', '**sea of free electrons**,' etc.

Module C3 — The Periodic Table

Superconductors and Transition Metals

Q1 Draw lines to match the transition metal to the process it catalyses.

iron   converting natural oils into fats

nickel   ammonia production

Q2 Complete the passage below by circling the correct word(s) from each pair.

> Most metals are in the transition block found **at the left** / **in the middle** of the periodic table.
> They generally have high **densities** / **volatility, low** / **high** melting points and are **good** / **poor**
> conductors of heat and electricity. Their compounds are **colourful** / **shiny** and, like the metals
> themselves, are often effective **fuels** / **catalysts**.

Q3 Under normal conditions **all** metals have **electrical resistance**.

a) Describe how electrical resistance causes energy to be wasted.

....

....

b) What is a superconductor? ....

c) Give three possible uses of superconducting wires.

1. ....

2. ....

3. ....

d) Explain a drawback of using today's superconductors.

....

....

Q4 'Colourful chemical gardens' can be made by sprinkling
transition metal salts into **sodium silicate solution**.
Transition metal silicate crystals grow upwards as shown.

sodium silicate solution

transition metal silicates

a) Why do you think transition metal salts are used?

....

b) Suggest three colours that you would be likely to see in the garden if iron(II) sulfate,
iron(III) chloride and copper(II) sulfate salts are used.

....

Thermal Decomposition and Precipitation

Q1 Draw lines to match the type of reaction with its description.

thermal decomposition

when a substance breaks down into simpler substances when heated

precipitation

where two solutions react and an insoluble solid is formed

Q2 Neil heats some **green** copper carbonate, $CuCO_3$. He is left with a **black** solid.

a) How can Neil tell that a reaction has taken place?

....

b) What type of reaction has taken place? ....

c) Write a word equation for this reaction.

....

d) Describe how you could **test** for **carbon dioxide**.

....

....

Q3 Write **balanced symbol equations** for the thermal decomposition of the following substances.

a) zinc carbonate, $ZnCO_3$

....

b) iron(II) carbonate, $FeCO_3$

....

c) copper(II) carbonate, $CuCO_3$

....

d) manganese(II) carbonate, $MnCO_3$

....

Thermal Decomposition and Precipitation

Q4   Clear, blue **copper(II) sulfate solution** and clear, colourless **sodium hydroxide** solution were mixed. The liquid went cloudy and pale blue. After a while a **pale blue solid** was left at the bottom and the liquid was **clear** again.

a)   What type of reaction has occurred? ....

b)   Name the blue solid formed.

....

c)   Write a balanced symbol equation for this reaction.

....

d)   Write a symbol equation to show the formation of the pale blue solid.

....

Q5   Cilla adds a few drops of **NaOH** solution to solutions of different **metal compounds**.

a)   Complete her table of results.

Compound	Metal Cation	Colour of Precipitate
copper(II) sulfate		blue
iron(II) sulfate		
iron(III) chloride	Fe^{3+}	
copper(II) chloride		

b)   Write a balanced symbol equation for the reaction of copper(II) chloride with sodium hydroxide.

....

c)   Complete the balanced ionic equation for the reaction of iron(II) ions with hydroxide ions.

These ionic equations should only show the ions involved in the formation of the precipitate.

Fe^{2+} + ... OH$^-$ → ....

d)   Write a balanced ionic equation for the reaction of **iron(III) ions** with hydroxide ions.

....

e)   Explain how this type of reaction could be used to help identify unknown metal ions.

....

....

....

Mixed Questions — Module C3

Q1 Hydrogen atoms can exist as three **isotopes** — ¹H (hydrogen), ²H (deuterium) and ³H (tritium).

a) What is an isotope?

....

b) Complete the table.

isotope	number of protons	number of neutrons	number of electrons
¹H			
²H			
³H			

c) The atomic number is often left out of the isotope symbol.
For instance, it is acceptable to write ¹²C for carbon-12 rather than $^{12}_{6}$C.

   i) Define the term **atomic number**.

....

   ii) Explain why the atomic number can be left out of the isotope symbol.

....

Q2 **Lithium** is a metallic element in **Group 1** of the periodic table.

a) Draw a diagram to show the electronic arrangement in a lithium atom.

Use the periodic table to help you.

b) Explain how lithium ions usually form.

....

c) **Fluorine** is in **Group 7** of the periodic table. Its electronic arrangement is shown below.

   i) Draw a diagram to show the electronic arrangement in a fluoride **ion**.

   ii) Give the chemical formula for the compound that forms between lithium and fluorine.

....

   iii) What type of bonding is involved in this compound?

....

Mixed Questions — Module C3

Q3   The table below gives some data for five **elements**.

Element	Melting point (°C)	Density (g/cm³)	Conducts electricity as solid?	Oxide of element	
				Colour (at RTP)	State (at RTP)
A	1455	8.9	Yes	Green	Solid
B	44	1.82	No	White	Solid
C	3550	3.51	No	Colourless	Gas
D	1535	7.86	Yes	Red	Solid
E	98	0.97	Yes	White	Solid

a)   Two of the elements are transition elements. Identify them and explain your answer.

....

....

b)   Give a use for one named transition element.

Transistion element: ....   Use: ....

Q4   **Aluminium** is extracted from its ore by **electrolysis**.

a)   What is electrolysis?

....

b)   The aluminium ions are attracted to the negative cathode.

i)   Explain what happens to the aluminium ions at the cathode.

....

ii)   Complete a balanced half-equation for the reaction that takes place.

Al^{3+} + ... → ....

c)   Oxygen ions are attracted to the anode.
Complete a balanced half-equation for the reaction there.

$2O^{2-}$ → .... + ...

d)   Electrolysis is a redox reaction. Explain what this means.

....

e)   In order to electrolyse aluminium oxide, it is dissolved in molten cryolite.
Explain why this is more cost-effective than just melting the aluminium oxide.

....

....

Module C3 — The Periodic Table

Mixed Questions — Module C3

Q5 The diagram shows the apparatus used to react **chlorine** with **magnesium**.

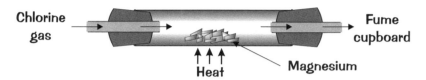

Chlorine gas → Fume cupboard

Heat ↑ ↑ ↑ — Magnesium

a) Why is it not possible to use the same apparatus to react iodine with magnesium?

....

b) Complete the chemical equation for the reaction: **Mg + Cl$_2$ →** ....

c) What type of bonding is present in the product? ....

d) Draw a dot and cross diagram to show the formation of magnesium chloride from magnesium and chlorine atoms.

e) Solid magnesium chloride does not conduct electricity. However, when magnesium chloride is dissolved in water or is molten it does conduct electricity. Explain these facts.

....

....

Q6 Metals are good **electrical conductors**. Explain why, using ideas about structure and bonding.

....

....

....

Q7 Iodine has a **simple molecular structure**.

a) What type of bonding binds the iodine atoms together in each molecule? ....

b) Explain why iodine has a low melting point.

....

....

c) Predict whether iodine is likely to be able to conduct electricity. Justify your prediction.

....

....

Acids and Bases

Q1   Define the following terms.

   a)   Acid ....

   b)   Base ....

   c)   Alkali ....

Q2 a)   Which is the correct word equation for a **neutralisation reaction**? Circle your answer.

       salt + acid → base + water   acid + base → salt + water

                      acid + water → base + salt

   b)   Which of the ions, $\boxed{\textbf{H}^+ \text{ or } \textbf{OH}^-}$, is found in the largest quantity in:

      i)   acidic solutions?   ....

      ii) alkaline solutions?   ....

      iii) a solution with a pH of 10?   ....

      iv) lemon juice?   ....

Q3   **Indigestion** is caused by too much acid in the stomach.
       Antacid tablets contain bases which neutralise the excess acid.

   Joey wanted to test whether some antacid tablets really did **neutralise acid**. He added a tablet to some hydrochloric acid, stirred it until it dissolved and tested the pH of the solution. Further tests were carried out after dissolving a second, third and fourth tablet.
   His results are shown in the table.

Number of Tablets	pH
0	1
1	2
2	3
3	7
4	9

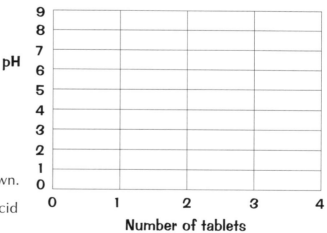

pH against no. of tablets added to acid

   a) **i)**   Plot a graph of the results on the grid shown.

      ii) Describe how the pH changes when antacid tablets are added to the acid.

      ....

      iii) How many tablets were needed to neutralise the acid? ....

   b)   Joey tested another brand of tablets and found that **two** tablets neutralised the same volume of acid. On the graph, sketch the results you might expect for these tablets.

Acids and Bases

Q4 Complete the following sentences with a single word.

a) Solutions which are not acidic or alkaline are said to be ....

b) Universal indicator is a combination of different coloured ....

c) When a substance is neutral it has a pH of ....

Q5 Ants' stings hurt because of the **formic acid** they release. The pH measurements of some household substances are given in the table.

SUBSTANCE	pH
lemon juice	4
baking soda	9
caustic soda	14
soap powder	11

a) Describe how you could test the formic acid to find its pH value.

....

b) Suggest a substance from the list that could be used to relieve the discomfort of an ant sting. Explain your answer.

....

....

c) Explain why **universal indicator** only gives an **estimate** of the pH of a substance.

....

Q6 Modern industry uses thousands of tonnes of **sulfuric acid** per day.

a) The pie chart shows the major uses of the sulfuric acid produced by a particular plant. What is the **main use** of the sulfuric acid from this plant?

....

Fibres 9%
Detergents 11%
Paints and Pigments 15%
Other Chemicals 16%
Fertilisers 32%
Other Uses 17%

b) Give two uses of sulfuric acid in the car manufacturing industry.

1. .... 2. ....

c) Which of the following compounds found in fertilisers is manufactured from sulfuric acid?

ammonium nitrate   **ammonium sulfate**   **ammonium phosphate**   **potassium nitrate**

d) Describe how sulfuric acid is used in the preparation of metal surfaces.

....

....

Top Tips: Ahh... acids and bases. They pop up everywhere. And I mean EVERYWHERE. The chemistry lab, the human body, vehicles, poisons and antidotes, even in the kitchen sink.

Module C4 — Chemical Economics

Reactions of Acids

Q1 Fill in the blanks to complete the word equations for
acids reacting with **metal oxides** and **metal hydroxides**.

a) hydrochloric acid + lead oxide → .... chloride + water

b) nitric acid + copper hydroxide → copper .... + water

c) sulfuric acid + zinc oxide → zinc sulfate + ...

d) hydrochloric acid + ... oxide → nickel .... + ...

e) .... acid + copper oxide → .... nitrate + ...

f) sulfuric acid + ... hydroxide → sodium .... + ...

Q2 a) Put a tick in the box next to any of the sentences below that are **true**.

i) Alkalis are bases which can't dissolve in water. ☐

ii) Acids react with metal oxides to form a salt and water. ☐

iii) Hydrogen gas is formed when an acid reacts with an alkali. ☐

iv) Salts and water are formed when acids react with metal hydroxides. ☐

v) Calcium hydroxide is an acid that dissolves in water. ☐

b) Use the formulas below to write **symbol equations** for two acid / base reactions.

H_2SO_4 H_2O CuO H_2O $NaCl$ HCl $CuSO_4$ $NaOH$

1. ....

2. ....

Q3 **Ammonia** can be neutralised by **nitric acid** to form **ammonium nitrate**.

a) Circle the correct formula for ammonia below.

NH_4NO_3 NH_4Cl NH_3 NH_2 NH_4

b) Write down the symbol equation for the reaction between ammonia and nitric acid.

....

c) How is this neutralisation reaction different from most neutralisation reactions?

....

d) Why is ammonium nitrate a particularly good fertiliser?

....

Module C4 — Chemical Economics

Reactions of Acids

Q4 a) Complete the following equations.

    i) H_2SO_4 + ... $\rightarrow$ $CuSO_4$ + H_2O

    ii) $2HNO_3$ + MgO $\rightarrow$ $Mg(NO_3)_2$ + ...

    iii) .... + KOH $\rightarrow$ KCl + H_2O

    iv) 2HCl + ... $\rightarrow$ $ZnCl_2$ + H_2O

    v) H_2SO_4 + 2NaOH $\rightarrow$ .... + ...

b) **Balance** the following acid/base reactions.

i)   NaOH + H_2SO_4 $\rightarrow$ Na_2SO_4 + H_2O

ii) $Mg(OH)_2$ + HNO_3 $\rightarrow$ $Mg(NO_3)_2$ + H_2O

iii) NH_3 + H_3PO_4 $\rightarrow$ $(NH_4)_3PO_4$

Q5   **Acids** react with **metal carbonates** in neutralisation reactions.

a) Complete the following word equations.

    i) hydrochloric acid + ... carbonate $\rightarrow$

         copper .... + water + ...

    ii) .... acid + magnesium .... $\rightarrow$

         .... nitrate + ... + carbon dioxide

    iii) sulfuric acid + lithium carbonate $\rightarrow$ .... + ...+ ....

b) Complete and balance the following symbol equations.

    i) .... HCl + $CaCO_3$ $\rightarrow$ $CaCl_2$ + ... + CO_2

    ii) H_2SO_4 + ... $\rightarrow$ Na_2SO_4 + ... + ...

    iii) .... + ... $\rightarrow$ $Ca(NO_3)_2$ + H_2O + CO_2

    iv) .... + Na_2CO_3 $\rightarrow$ .... NaCl + ... + ...

c) Keith wants to confirm that the gas released when he reacts calcium carbonate with hydrochloric acid is **carbon dioxide**. Outline an **experimental procedure** he could use to test the gas.

....

....

Relative Formula Mass

Q1 What are the **relative atomic masses** (A_r) of the following:

a) Magnesium ....

b) Neon ....

c) Oxygen ....

d) Hydrogen ....

e) C ....

f) Cu ....

g) K ....

h) Ca ....

i) Cl ....

Q2 Identify the elements A, B and C.

> Element A has an A_r of 4.
> Element B has an A_r 3 times that of element A.
> Element C has an A_r 4 times that of element A.

Element A = ...

Element B = ...

Element C = ...

Q3 a) Explain how the **relative formula mass** of a **compound** is calculated.

....

b) What are the **relative formula masses** (M_r) of the following:

i) Water, H_2O ....

ii) Potassium hydroxide, KOH ....

iii) Nitric acid, HNO_3 ....

iv) Ammonium nitrate, NH_4NO_3 ....

v) Calcium nitrate, $Ca(NO_3)_2$ ....

vi) Iron(III) hydroxide, $Fe(OH)_3$ ....

Q4 The equation below shows a reaction between element X and water. The sum of the M_r of the **reactants** is **114**. What is element X?

$$2X + 2H_2O \rightarrow 2XOH + H_2$$

....

....

Calculating Masses in Reactions

Q1   Anna burns **10 g** of **magnesium** in air to produce **magnesium oxide** (MgO).

   a)   Write out the **balanced equation** for this reaction.

   ....

   b)   Calculate the mass of **magnesium oxide** that's produced.

   ....

   ....

   ....

Q2   What mass of **sodium** is needed to make **2 g** of **sodium oxide**? $4Na + O_2 \rightarrow 2Na_2O$

   ....

   ....

   ....

Q3   **Aluminium** and **iron oxide** (Fe_2O_3) react together to produce **aluminium oxide** (Al_2O_3) and **iron**.

   a)   Write out the **balanced equation** for this reaction.

   ....

   b)   What **mass** of iron is produced from **20 g** of iron oxide?

   ....

   ....

   ....

Q4   When heated, **limestone** ($CaCO_3$) decomposes to form **calcium oxide** (CaO) and **carbon dioxide**.

   How many **kilograms** of limestone are needed to make **100 kilograms** of **calcium oxide**?

   The calculation is exactly
   the same — just use 'kg'
   instead of 'g'.   ....

   ....

   ....

Calculating Masses in Reactions

Q5 **Iron oxide** is reduced to **iron** inside a blast furnace using carbon. There are **three** stages involved.

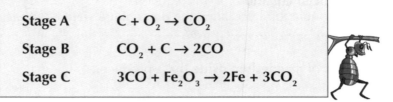

Stage A	$C + O_2 \rightarrow CO_2$
Stage B	$CO_2 + C \rightarrow 2CO$
Stage C	$3CO + Fe_2O_3 \rightarrow 2Fe + 3CO_2$

a) If **10 g** of **carbon** are used in stage B, and all the carbon monoxide produced gets used in stage C, what **mass** of CO_2 is produced in **stage C**?

....

....

Work out the mass of CO at the end of stage B first.

....

....

b) Suggest how the CO_2 might be used after stage C.

....

Look at where CO_2 is used.

Q6 **Sodium sulfate** (Na_2SO_4) is made by reacting **sodium hydroxide** (NaOH) with **sulfuric acid** (H_2SO_4). **Water** is also produced.

a) Write out the **balanced equation** for this reaction.

....

b) What mass of **sodium hydroxide** is needed to make **75 g** of **sodium sulfate**?

....

....

....

....

c) What mass of **water** is formed when **50 g** of **sulfuric acid** reacts?

....

....

....

....

Percentage Yield

Q1 James wanted to produce **silver chloride** (AgCl). He added a carefully measured mass of silver nitrate to an excess of dilute hydrochloric acid. An **insoluble white salt** formed.

a) Write down the formula for calculating the **percentage yield** of a reaction.

b) James calculated that he should get 2.7 g of silver chloride, but he only got 1.2 g. What was the **percentage yield**?

....

....

Q2 Explain how the following factors can affect the **percentage yield**.

a) Heating ....

....

b) Filtration (when you want to keep the liquid) ....

....

c) Transferring liquids ....

....

d) Evaporation ....

....

Q3 Aaliya and Natasha mixed together barium chloride ($BaCl_2$) and sodium sulfate (Na_2SO_4) in a beaker. An **insoluble** substance formed. They **filtered** the solution to obtain the solid substance, and then transferred the solid to a clean piece of **filter paper** and left it to dry.

a) Aaliya calculated that they should produce a yield of **15 g** of barium sulfate. However, after completing the experiment they found they had only obtained **6 g**.

Calculate the **percentage yield** for this reaction.

....

....

b) Suggest two reasons why their actual yield was lower than their predicted yield.

1. ....

2. ....

Fertilisers

Q1   Choose from the words to fill in the blanks below.

non-essential	sodium	proteins	yield	growth
phosphorus	carbohydrates	previous	essential	

Fertilisers are used to increase crop .... They provide plants with

.... elements needed for ...., making crops grow

faster and bigger. These elements include nitrogen, ... and potassium.

Nitrogen is used in plants to make .... Fertilisers replace elements in

the soil that a .... crop could have used up.

Q2   Sophie is concerned about the amount of **fertiliser** that gets washed into **rivers**.

a)   Circle any of the following compounds that can be used as fertilisers.

ammonium nitrate   potassium nitrate   nitric acid   copper carbonate   ammonium phosphate
urea   oxygen

b)   Sophie suggests trapping the fertiliser compounds in **insoluble** pellets. Why is this idea flawed?

....

Q3   Tamsin prepares **ammonium sulfate** in the lab using the apparatus shown
in the diagram. She finds that she needs 12.6 cm³ of sulfuric acid to **just**
change the colour of the methyl orange indicator from yellow to red.

sulfuric acid

a)   Suggest what piece of apparatus Tamsin used to
accurately measure 25.0 cm³ of ammonia solution.

....

b)   Name the apparatus shown in the diagram that's used
to add the sulfuric acid into the ammonia solution.

25.0 cm³ of ammonia
solution + methyl
orange indicator

....

white tile

c)   What type of reaction is occurring? ....

Tamsin repeats the experiment to obtain **pure** crystals of ammonium sulfate.

d)   What important **difference** must she make to her experimental procedure to produce
pure ammonium sulfate?

....

e)   What volume of sulfuric acid must she add? ....

f)   How can Tamsin get ammonium sulfate crystals from her ammonium sulfate solution?

....

....

Module C4 — Chemical Economics

Fertilisers

Q4   Number the following stages 1– 6 to describe the process of **eutrophication**.

- [ ] There is a rapid growth of algae, called an 'algal bloom'.
- [ ] Plants die because they don't receive enough light.
- [ ] The amounts of nitrates and phosphates in the water increase.
- [ ] Fish and other living organisms start to die.
- [ ] Excess fertiliser runs off fields into rivers and streams.
- [ ] Decomposers feed off the dead plants, using up all the oxygen in the water.

Q5   Calculate the **relative formula masses**, M_r, of the following fertilisers.

a)   potassium nitrate, KNO_3 ....

b)   ammonium sulfate, $(NH_4)_2SO_4$ ....

c)   ammonium phosphate, $(NH_4)_3PO_4$ ....

Q6   Calculate the **percentage mass** of nitrogen in the following compounds.

Use the equation
$$\% \text{ mass} = \frac{(A_r \times n)}{M_r} \times 100$$

a)   ammonium nitrate, NH_4NO_3

....

b)   urea, $CO(NH_2)_2$

....

Q7   Farmer Freda wants to give a field of crops exactly **50 kg** of potassium.

Start by calculating the % mass of potassium in potassium nitrate.

a)   What mass of potassium nitrate fertiliser, KNO_3, should she apply?

....

....

b)   In applying the potassium nitrate in **a)**, what mass of **nitrogen** will also have been provided?

....

....

Q8   Suggest **three** pieces of advice on the use of fertilisers that could be given to farmers to help prevent **eutrophication**.

1. ....

2. ....

3. ....

The Haber Process

Q1 The Haber process is used to make **ammonia**.

a) The equation for the reaction is

$$N_2 + 3H_2 \rightleftharpoons 2NH_3$$

    i) Name the reactants in the forward reaction ....

    ii) Which side of the equation has more molecules? ....

b) Give a **use** of ammonia.

....

Q2 The **industrial conditions** for the Haber process are carefully chosen.

a) What conditions are used? Tick one box.

☐ 1000 atmospheres, 450 °C	☐ 200 atmospheres, 1000 °C	☐ 450 atmospheres, 200 °C	☐ 200 atmospheres, 450 °C

b) Give two reasons why the pressure used is chosen.

    1. ....

    2. ....

Q3 In the Haber process, the forward reaction is **exothermic**.

a) What effect will raising the temperature have on the **amount** of ammonia formed?

....

b) Explain why a high temperature is used industrially.

....

c) What happens to the leftover nitrogen and hydrogen? ....

Q4 The Haber process uses an **iron catalyst**.

a) What effect does this have on the % yield? ....

b) Iron catalysts are cheap. What effect does using one have on the **cost** of producing the ammonia? Explain your answer.

....

....

Top Tips: Changing the conditions in a reversible reaction to get more product sounds great, but don't forget that these conditions might be too difficult or expensive for factories to produce, or they might make the reaction too slow to be profitable.

Minimising the Cost of Production

Q1   Use the following words to complete the blanks.

yield	sufficient	optimum	rate	recycled	lowest

.... conditions are chosen to give the .... production

cost per kg of product. This may mean that the conditions used do not have the

highest .... of reaction or the highest percentage ....

of product. However, both the rate and the yield must be high enough to give a

.... daily yield of product. A low percentage yield is acceptable if the

starting materials can be .... and reacted again.

Q2   Explain how the following affect the **production costs** of making a new substance.

a)   Catalysts ....

....

b)   Recycling raw materials ....

....

c)   Automation ....

....

d)   High temperatures ....

....

Q3   A pharmaceutical company tests two production processes for producing a new drug. Rupert records both the total **production cost** and the total **yield** for each process over a one-week period.

a)   Calculate the cost per g of drug for each process.

....

....

....

....

....

b)   Suggest why the company decides to use process B, even though it has a higher production cost.

....

Detergents and Dry-Cleaning

Q1 Match the following terms to their correct descriptions.

solvent

A substance that's dissolved in a liquid.

solution

A liquid mixture made from dissolving a substance in a liquid.

solute

A liquid that can dissolve a substance.

Q2 Some fabrics need to be **dry-cleaned**.

a) What is dry-cleaning? ....

b) Name **one** solvent commonly used in dry-cleaning. ....

c) Give two reasons why it is necessary to dry-clean some clothes rather than using a detergent.

1. ....

2. ....

Q3 The diagram shows a detergent molecule.

a) Complete the diagram by labelling the **hydrophilic** and **hydrophobic** sections of the molecule.

....

b) Which section of the molecule is attracted to:

i) water molecules? ....

ii) grease and oil? ....

c) The first detergents used by humans thousands of years ago were soaps made from fats.

i) What disadvantage do soaps have when used in **hard water** areas? ....

ii) What raw material are modern synthetic detergents made from? ....

Q4 Fill in blanks using the appropriate words below.

| water | stain | intermolecular | disperse |
| intramolecular | pull | grease | sugar | react |

Detergents work by helping dirt to .... in water. Normally oil or

.... stains do not mix with water. The hydrophobic tail attaches

to the fat molecules in the stain with .... forces. The hydrophilic

head is surrounded by .... molecules outside the stain.

The movement of the washing machine helps the detergent molecules to

.... away droplets of oil into the water, leaving the fabric clean.

Detergents and Dry-Cleaning

Q5 Many modern detergents used for washing clothes are **'biological'**.

a) What is the difference between biological and non-biological detergents?

....

b) Why do biological detergents become less effective at temperatures above 40 °C?

....

c) Circle the types of stain below that biological detergents should be particularly effective at cleaning.

paint   blood   grass   tomato ketchup   engine oil

Q6 Felicity works for a chemical company that is developing a new washing powder. She tests five different powders and records their cleaning effectiveness at different temperatures and against a range of different stains. She uses a scale of 1 (poor) to 10 (excellent).

a) Which powder is best at cleaning grass stains at 40 °C?

....

b) Which powders could be biological detergents? Give a reason for your answer.

....

....

....

		Washing powder				
		A	B	C	D	E
Effectiveness	at 40 °C	9	3	5	7	7
	at 60 °C	3	3	9	8	4
	Against tomato stains (at 40 °C)	8	1	5	4	10
	Against grass stains (at 40 °C)	8	4	5	7	3

Q7 Emily is trying to decide what temperature is best to wash her clothes at.

a) Why are **high** temperatures usually best for washing clothes?

....

b) Why shouldn't you wash clothes made from the following materials at high temperatures?

i) Wool ....

ii) Nylon ....

c) Emily's friend says, 'Washing clothes at high temperatures is environmentally unfriendly.' Explain why.

....

....

Detergents and Dry-Cleaning

Q8 Simon sets up a test to find which of four different washing powders is most effective.
He cuts a white cotton cloth into four pieces and stains each one with a different substance.

The diagram shows the four different washes that he has planned.

Describe why Simon's experiment is **not** a fair test.

....

....

....

| Egg yolk Powder A | Blackcurrant Powder B |
| Curry Powder C | Engine oil Powder D |

Q9 Use these words to complete the blanks.

| ionic | intramolecular | solute | solvent | detergents |
| intermolecular | surrounded | covalent | solution | bonds |

When a solid is dissolved in a liquid, ... forces occur between

the liquid molecules and the solid particles. These forces help to break

.... between the solid particles and the solid breaks up. A solid is

dissolved when its particles are completely .... by liquid molecules.

.... are used to help water dissolve substances. Some substances

will not dissolve in water at all and another .... is required.

Q10 A chemical company is testing three new solvents for dry-cleaning.

a) What mass of solvent A is needed to dissolve 50 g of paint?

....

....

....

	Solvent		
	A	**B**	**C**
Cost per 100 g (£)	0.40	0.15	0.20
Solubility of paint (g per 100 g of solvent)	12.1	0.1	10.3

b) Which solvent would you expect to form the strongest intermolecular forces with paint molecules?
Explain your answer.

....

c) Which solvent would you choose to buy if you were a buyer for a dry-cleaning company?
Explain your choice.

....

....

Module C4 — Chemical Economics

Chemical Production

Q1 Suggest whether **continuous** or **batch** production would be used to make the following chemicals.

a) Perfumes ....

b) Sulfuric acid ....

c) Ammonia ....

d) Paints ....

Q2 Widely used chemicals are often produced by **continuous production**.

a) Circle the correct words to complete the following sentences.

Continuous production is often used for the small-scale / large-scale production of chemicals.
It's highly automated / labour-intensive, which means that there are low / high labour costs.
Continuous production means that products of a high / low consistency can be produced with
a high / low risk of contamination.

b) State two **disadvantages** of continuous production.

1. ....

2. ....

Q3 **Batch production** is used to produce specialist chemicals.

a) Use these words to complete the blanks about batch production.

inflexible   high   small   contamination   large   versatile   low

Batch production is often used for manufacturing .... quantities of
specialist chemicals. The advantages of batch production are that the plant is
.... (allowing for many different products to be made), and that the costs
of plant equipment are .... Disadvantages of batch production include
the .... labour costs and the increased risk of ....

b) Why are **pharmaceutical drugs** usually manufactured using batch production?

....

c) In the context of batch production, what is '**downtime**'?

....

....

Chemical Production

Q4   Compounds used in pharmaceutical drugs are often extracted from **plants**.

a)   Describe the following steps in the extraction process.

A   B   C

Step A ....

Step B ....

Step C ....

b)   New drugs may be tested on animals before being sold.

i)   Give one argument for and one argument against testing new drugs on **animals**.

For ....

Against ....

ii)   After animal testing, why are **human trials** of drugs also necessary?

....

Q5   Tony decides his pharmaceutical company should develop and manufacture a new drug.

a)   Suggest one thing that Tony needs to research before developing a new drug.

....

b)   Give two reasons why the **research** and **development** of new pharmaceutical drugs is expensive.

1. ....

2. ....

c)   Give two reasons why the **manufacturing** process of pharmaceutical drugs is expensive.

1. ....

2. ....

d)   Explain why it might be a long time before Tony gets back his initial investment.

....

....

....

Allotropes of Carbon

Q1 **Diamond** is an allotrope of carbon.

a) Circle the correct words to complete the sentences below about diamond.

Diamond has a **simple molecular / giant covalent** structure. Each carbon atom in diamond forms **three / four** bonds with neighbouring atoms. Diamond is **soft / hard** and has a **low / high** melting point, which makes it ideal for use in **lubricants / cutting tools**.

b) Why is diamond **unable** to conduct electricity?

....

c) Name two properties of diamond that make it useful for **jewellery**.

1. .... 2. ....

Q2 **Graphite** is another allotrope of carbon.

a) Choose from these words to complete the blanks below.

| four | red | tools | lubricant | tightly | three | high |
| low | black | loosely | slide | delocalised |

Graphite is made of layers of carbon that are held .... together. It is .... in colour. Within the layers, each carbon atom forms .... covalent bonds. These strong covalent bonds give graphite a .... melting point. Between the layers there is only a weak attraction. This enables the layers to .... easily over each other, which makes it useful as a ....

b) Explain why graphite is **able** to conduct electricity.

....

....

c) Give two reasons why graphite is used in pencil leads.

1. ....

2. ....

Top Tips: There's more than one allotrope of carbon you've got to know about and each one is well suited to its uses. You wouldn't use diamonds in your tennis racket after all. Well, unless you were exceptionally rich, and then you could have diamonds on the soles of your shoes as well.

Allotropes of Carbon

Q3 The diagram shows a molecule of **buckminsterfullerene**.

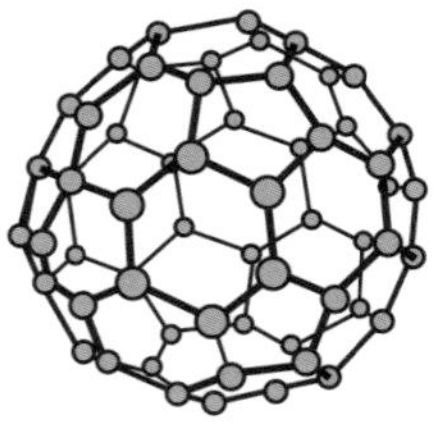

a) What is the **molecular formula** of buckminsterfullerene? ....

b) How many covalent bonds does each carbon atom form? ....

c) Can buckminsterfullerene conduct electricity? Explain your answer.

....

....

d) Fullerenes can be used to 'cage' other molecules. Give a potential use for this technology.

....

Q4 Nanoparticles are really tiny particles, between 1 and 100 nanometres across.

a) How many nanometres are there in **1 mm**?

$1\,m = 1 \times 10^9\,nm$

....

....

b) Describe an example of a nanoparticle having very different properties to the 'bulk' chemical.

....

c) Explain how nanoparticles are useful in producing industrial **catalysts**.

....

....

Q5 Fullerenes can be joined together to make nanotubes.

a) What are nanotubes?

Piccadilly

....

b) Give **two** properties of nanotubes that make them useful in **electrical circuits**.

....

....

c) Give a property of nanotubes that makes them useful in **tennis rackets**.

....

Water Purity

Q1   There are limited water resources in the UK.

a)   Which one of the following water resources is a source of 'groundwater'? Circle your answer.

reservoirs   aquifers   rivers   lakes

b)   Name three important uses of water in **industrial processes**.

1. ....

2. ....

3. ....

Q2   Suggest **one** way that water could be **conserved** by:

a)   a water company

....

b)   domestic water users

....

Q3   Water is **treated** before it reaches our homes.

a)   Number the stages 1–4 to show the correct order of the processes in a **water treatment** plant.

☐ Sedimentation   ☐ Filtration through sand beds

☐ Chlorination   ☐ Filtration through a wire mesh

b)   Why are two filtration processes needed? ....

....

c)   Name a chemical used in the sedimentation process. ....

d)   Why are the purification processes unable to remove impurities such as ammonium nitrate?

....

e)   Why is chlorination used in the purification process?

....

Q4   Helen's house has an **old plumbing system**. She's concerned about **pollutants** in the tap water.

a)   What form of pollution in the tap water could be caused by the plumbing system?

....

b)   Helen's water supply comes from a reservoir located in an area of intensive agriculture.
Suggest **two** other forms of pollutant which could be present in the tap water.

....

Water Purity

Q5   **Sodium sulfate** reacts with **barium chloride** in a precipitation reaction.

a)   What is a **precipitation reaction**?

....

b)   Complete the word equation for this reaction.

sodium sulfate + barium chloride → barium .... + ...

c)   Complete and balance the symbol equation for this reaction.

Na_2SO_4 + ... → .... + ...$NaCl$

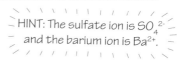

HINT: The sulfate ion is SO_4^{2-} and the barium ion is Ba^{2+}.

Q6   Sam creates a flow chart as a key to help her identify **halide anions** present in a sample of water.

a)   Finish the flow chart by completing the empty boxes.

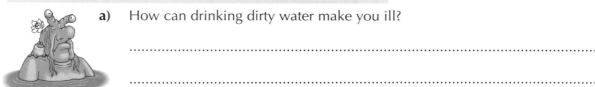

Water sample → Add dilute nitric acid → [   ] → White precipitate → [   ]
→ [   ] → Br^- ions
→ [   ] → I^- ions

b)   Complete the following symbol equations involved in testing for halide ions.

    i) $AgNO_3 + KCl →$ .... $+ KNO_3$ iii) $Ag^+ + Br^- →$ ....

    ii) .... + ... $→ AgI + NaNO_3$

Q7   People in developing countries often can't get **clean water**.

a)   How can drinking dirty water make you ill?

....

....

b)   Suggest how developing countries can help ensure everyone has a supply of clean water.

....

....

Q8   Some countries get fresh water by **distilling** seawater.

a)   Give **one** advantage of this method.

....

b)   Give **two** disadvantages of this method.

....

....

Module C4 — Chemical Economics

Mixed Questions — Module C4

Q1 Three forms of the element carbon are shown in the diagram.

● carbon atoms

a) Identify the different forms by name.

R .... S .... T ....

b) Form **R** has a melting point of 3652 °C. Form **S** has a melting point of 3550 °C.

i) Explain why forms R and S have very high melting points.
You should mention structure and bonding in your answer.

....

....

ii) Predict whether the melting point of form **T** will be greater than, the same as, or lower
than those of the other two forms. Justify your answer.

....

....

Q2 Orwell reacted silicon with chlorine to produce the liquid silicon chloride ($SiCl_4$).

a) Calculate the **relative formula mass** of silicon chloride.

....

b) Calculate the **percentage mass** of chlorine in silicon chloride.

....

c) Write down the **balanced symbol equation** for the reaction.

....

d) How much chlorine would Orwell need to react with **2.8 g of silicon**?

....

....

e) Orwell predicted he would obtain 17.0 g of silicon chloride, however he only obtained 13.0 g.
Calculate the **percentage yield** for this reaction.

....

f) Suggest two ways in which some of the product may have been lost from the reaction container.
(There was no filtration involved in the process.)

....

....

Mixed Questions — Module C4

Q3   The diagram shows the **pH scale**.

| 1 | 2 | 3 | 4 | 5 | 6 | 7 | 8 | 9 | 10 | 11 | 12 | 13 |

↑ black coffee   ↑ magnesium hydroxide

a)   The pH values of black coffee and magnesium hydroxide are marked on the diagram.

    i) Is black coffee neutral, acidic or alkaline? ....

    ii) Is magnesium hydroxide neutral, acidic or alkaline? ....

b)   Indigestion is caused by excess acid in the stomach. Magnesium hydroxide, $Mg(OH)_2$, is used in indigestion remedies. Explain how magnesium hydroxide can help with indigestion.

....

Q4   Some solid **magnesium oxide** was added to **HCl** solution in a test tube. The reactants and the products are shown, but the equation is **not** balanced.

$$MgO\ (s)\ +\ HCl\ (aq)\ \rightarrow\ D\ (aq)\ +\ H_2O\ (l)$$

a)   **i)** Give the chemical formula of substance **D**. ....

    ii) What would be observed as the reaction **proceeded**?

....

b)   When solid magnesium oxide was added to a substance **S**, magnesium sulfate and water were formed. Identify S by name or formula. ....

c)   Describe a **chemical test** you could use to distinguish between a solution of magnesium sulfate and a solution of substance D.

....

....

Q5   **Detergents** are usually used in washing machines.

a)   Indicate whether the following statements are **true** or **false**.

                                                           True False

    i)   Detergents are always more effective at high temperatures.   ☐ ☐

    ii) Washing clothes at lower temperatures is more environmentally friendly. ☐ ☐

    iii) Most synthetic detergents are alkalis.   ☐ ☐

    iv) The hydrophobic end of detergent molecules bonds to grease molecules. ☐ ☐

b)   Explain why dry cleaning might remove a **paint stain** that a detergent failed to remove.

....

....

Mixed Questions — Module C4

Q6 The **cost** of producing ammonia in the Haber process depends on several factors.

a) Give **four factors** on which the cost of producing ammonia depends.

....

....

b) The temperature and pressure conditions for the Haber process could be described as
'**a compromise**'. With reference to these conditions explain what the 'compromise' is.

....

....

....

c) Suggest two reasons why ammonia is made using **continuous production**
rather than batch production.

....

....

Q7 **Fertilisers** dramatically increase the quantity and quality of crops.

a) Ammonium nitrate is a good fertiliser, because it contains two sources of nitrogen.

   i) Write a balanced equation to show the reaction of ammonia (NH_3) with nitric acid (HNO_3) to
   produce ammonium nitrate (NH_4NO_3).

   ....

   ii) This a neutralisation reaction. Explain why.

   ....

   iii) Why is nitrogen important to plants?

   ....

b) Explain how excess fertiliser on fields can kill fish in local rivers.

....

....

Q8 Explain why the following substances are added in the **water purification** process:

a) aluminium sulfate ....

....

b) chlorine gas ....

Module C4 — Chemical Economics

The Mole

Q1 a) **Complete** the following sentence.

> One mole of atoms or molecules of any substance will have a .... in
> grams equal to the .... for that substance.

b) What is the mass of each of the following?

  i) 2 moles of nitric acid, HNO_3. ....

  ii) 0.5 moles of calcium carbonate, $CaCO_3$. ....

  iii) 5.4 moles of magnesium hydroxide, $Mg(OH)_2$. ....

Q2 What is the **relative atomic mass** of an element?

....

....

Q3 a) Write down the formula for calculating the **number of moles in a given mass**.

b) How many **moles** are there in each of the following?

  i) 37 g of calcium hydroxide, $Ca(OH)_2$.

  ....

  ii) 112 g of sulfur dioxide, SO_2.

  ....

  iii) 200 g of copper oxide, CuO.

  ....

Q4 Calculate the **mass** of each of the following.

a) 0.75 moles of magnesium oxide, MgO.

....

b) 0.025 moles of lead chloride, $PbCl_2$.

....

c) 2 moles of ammonium sulfate, $(NH_4)_2SO_4$.

....

Reacting Masses and Empirical Formulas

Q1   Give the **empirical formula** for each of the following compounds.

a) $C_2H_4O_2$ ....

b) C_4H_8 ....

c) P_4O_{10} ....

Q2   Tim heats 3.2 g of copper with sulfur to form copper sulfide.

Complete the table to work out how much copper sulfide will be produced.
All the copper reacts to form copper sulfide.

Copper sulfide is the only product formed in this reaction.

Mass of copper / g	Mass of sulfur / g	Mass of copper sulfide / g
64	32	
32		
3.2		

Q3   Calculate the **empirical formula** of the compound formed when:

a)   20 g of calcium combines with 8 g of oxygen.

....

....

b)   5.4 g of aluminium combines with 9.6 g of sulfur.

....

....

Q4   An **oxide** of **sulfur** contains **60% oxygen**.

a)   What is the percentage of sulfur in the oxide?

....

b)   Calculate the empirical formula of the oxide.

....

....

Q5   A **carbonate** was found to contain **28.6% magnesium**, **14.3% carbon** and **57.1% oxygen**.
Work out the **empirical formula** of the compound.

....

....

....

Module C5 — How Much?

Electrolysis

Q1   Circle the correct word(s) in each pair to complete the passage below.

During electrolysis of an ionic compound, an electric current is passed through a molten or solid / **dissolved** substance, causing it to **decompose** / **melt**. Electrons are **given to** / **taken from** ions at the positive electrode and passed through the **external circuit** / **electrolyte** to the negative electrode, where they are **given to** / **taken from** other ions in the solution. Atoms or **molecules** / **ions** are formed and **discharged** / **insulated** from the solution.

Q2   **Sodium chloride solution** (brine) can electrolysed using the apparatus shown below.

a)   Complete the labelling of the diagram.

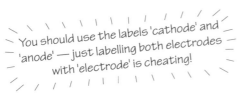
~ You should use the labels 'cathode' and 'anode' — just labelling both electrodes with 'electrode' is cheating!

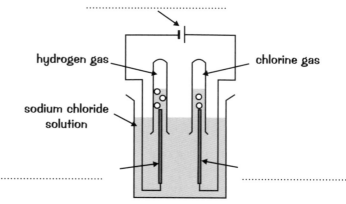
hydrogen gas   chlorine gas

sodium chloride solution

b)   Complete the symbol equation for the reaction at the positive electrode:

...... $Cl^- \rightarrow Cl_2 +$ ...... e^-

c)   What product would be different if the solution used was sodium nitrate?

....

Q3   Tick the correct boxes to show whether the following statements are **true** or **false**.

		True	False
a)	Electrons flow from the negative electrode to the positive electrode via ions in solution.	☐	☐
b)	Positive cations move to the negative electrode and lose electrons.	☐	☐
c)	Negative anions move to the positive electrode and give up electrons.	☐	☐
d)	A salt will **only** conduct an electric current when molten.	☐	☐

Q4   Complete and balance the following **half-equations**.

a)   At the cathode:

i) $K^+ +$ .... $\rightarrow K$

ii) $Pb^{2+} +$ .... $\rightarrow Pb$

iii) .... $+ 3e^- \rightarrow Al$

b)   At the anode:

i) $Br^- \rightarrow Br +$ ....

ii) .... $\rightarrow Cl + e^-$

iii) $O^{2-} \rightarrow$ ....

Electrolysis

Q5   Predict the elements formed during electrolysis for the remaining **molten** compounds in the table.

Compound	Product formed at the:	
	Negative electrode	Positive electrode
sodium chloride	sodium	chlorine
lead bromide		
copper chloride		
zinc oxide		
calcium oxide		

Q6   Roy electrolyses **potassium sulfate solution**, K_2SO_4.

a)   Give the formulas of the **four** ions present in this solution. ....

b)   i)   Which ion is discharged at the anode? Explain your answer.

....

ii)   Write a balanced symbol equation for this reaction.

....

c)   i)   Which ion is discharged at the cathode? Explain your answer.

....

ii)   Write a balanced symbol equation for this reaction.

....

d)   Suggest why the electrodes are made from graphite for the electrolysis of potassium sulfate.

....

Q7   Study the reactivity series and the table showing the products at the cathodes when different solutions of **ionic compounds** are electrolysed.

What do you notice about the substance released at the cathode and where it's found in the reactivity series?

Ionic Compound Solution	Product at Cathode
sodium nitrate	hydrogen
copper sulfate	copper
sodium iodide	hydrogen
potassium chloride	hydrogen
silver nitrate	silver

reactivity
potassium
sodium
calcium
carbon
zinc
iron
lead
hydrogen
copper
silver

....

....

Electrolysis

Q8 The table shows the **ions** present in solutions of some ionic compounds and the **products** formed when these solutions are electrolysed. Use this table to answer the following questions.

SOLUTION	IONS PRESENT	CATHODE	ANODE
calcium nitrate	Ca^{2+}, NO_3^-, H^+, OH^-	hydrogen	oxygen
copper chloride	Cu^{2+}, Cl^-, H^+, OH^-	copper	chlorine
sodium sulfate	Na^+, SO_4^{2-}, H^+, OH^-	hydrogen	oxygen
potassium bromide	K^+, Br^-, H^+, OH^-	hydrogen	bromine

a) Where do the H^+ and OH^- ions present in the solutions come from? ....

b) **i)** Give the formulas of two negative ions that are discharged **less** easily than the OH^- ion.

....

ii) Give the formulas of two negative ions that are discharged **more** easily than the OH^- ion.

....

c) **i)** Give the formula of a positive ion that is discharged more easily than an H^+ ion. ....

ii) Give the formulas of the positive ions that are discharged less easily than H^+ ions.

....

Q9 Andrew is electrolysing a solution of **copper(II) sulfate** ($CuSO_4$). He uses two **pure copper electrodes** both with a mass of 10 g. After about 5 minutes he notices that a fresh coating of copper had formed on one of the **electrodes**.

a) Describe what is happening at the:

i) positive electrode. ....

....

ii) negative electrode. ....

....

b) Write a balanced half-equation to show the reaction at:

i) the negative electrode: ....

ii) the positive electrode: ....

c) After 5 minutes he stops the electrolysis, and weighs the electrodes again.

Would you expect the total mass of the electrodes to be **more**, **less** or **the same**?
Explain your answer.

....

....

Electrolysis — Calculating Masses

Q1 Complete the table to show the amounts required to produce **1 mole** of each metal from its ions.

Metal ion	No. of moles of electrons	No. of faradays	No. of coulombs
Ca^{2+}			
K^+			
Al^{3+}			

Q2 a) Give two ways you could increase the amount of a substance produced during electrolysis.

1. ....

2. ....

b) Write down the formula for calculating the amount of charge transferred.

c) Calculate the charge transferred when:

i) 2.5 A has flowed for 15 s. ....

ii) 0.1 A has flowed for 30 mins. ....

d) Calculate the time (in minutes) 6 A needs to flow for to pass 4320 coulombs.

....

Q3 **Silver nitrate** was electrolysed for **40 minutes** using a current of **0.2 amps**.

a) Write the half-equation for the reaction at the **negative electrode**.

....

b) How many **coulombs** of charge flowed during the electrolysis?

....

c) How many **faradays** is this? ....

d) How many **moles** of silver were deposited at the cathode? ....

e) Calculate the **mass** of silver deposited at the cathode.

....

Top Tips: These calculations are HARD! The next page is full of similar questions, because, as you know, the only way to get good at sums is to practise, practise and then practise some more.

106

Electrolysis — Calculating Masses

Follow the steps given in the previous question to help you do the calculation.

Q4 Find the mass of zinc liberated if **6 amps** flows for **20 minutes** during the electrolysis of zinc chloride, $ZnCl_2$.

....

....

....

....

....

Q5 **Copper(II) sulfate**, $CuSO_4$, was electrolysed using a current of **0.4 A**. Follow these steps to calculate how long it would take to produce **0.32 g** of copper at the cathode.

a) Write a balanced half-equation for the reaction at the negative electrode.

....

b) How many faradays does it take to produce 1 mole of copper? ....

c) How many coulombs does it take to produce 1 mole of copper?

....

d) How many moles are there in 0.32 g of copper?

....

e) How many coulombs would give 0.32 g of copper?

....

f) How long would it take to produce 0.32 g of copper with a 0.4 A current? Give your answer in minutes.

Remember, $Q = I \times t$

....

Q6 Molten magnesium iodide, MgI_2, is electrolysed for **20 minutes**. The mass of magnesium liberated is **0.6 g**. What is the current used?

....

....

....

....

....

Module C5 — How Much?

Concentration

Q1 a) Write down the formula for calculating the **number of moles in a solution**.

b) Use the formula to calculate the number of moles in:

There are 1000 cm³ in 1 litre.

i) 50 cm³ of a 2 M solution. ....

ii) 250 cm³ of a 0.5 M solution. ....

iii) 550 cm³ of a 1.75 M solution. ....

c) **200 cm³** of a solution contains **0.25 moles** of iron hydroxide, $Fe(OH)_3$.
Calculate its **molar concentration**.

....

d) What **volume** of a 1.6 M solution of calcium hydroxide contains **2 moles** of calcium hydroxide?

....

Q2 Convert the concentration of the following solutions from **mol/dm³** to **g/dm³**.

a) **2 mol/dm³** sodium hydroxide, NaOH. ....

....

b) **0.1 mol/dm³** glucose, $C_6H_{12}O_6$. ....

....

Q3 Convert the concentration of the following solutions from **g/dm³** to **mol/dm³**.

a) **5.6 g/dm³** potassium hydroxide, KOH. ....

....

b) **21 g/dm³** sodium hydrogencarbonate solution, $NaHCO_3$. ....

....

Q4 Barry dissolved **8 g** of copper(II) sulfate ($CuSO_4$) in **500 cm³** of water.
Work out the concentration of this solution in **mol/dm³**.

....

....

....

Concentration

Q5   Cedric is testing substance X as a new **drug** for asthma. The drug is manufactured at a concentration of **1 M** and is then **diluted** before being given to patients.

a)   Explain why it is important that the drug given to patients is not:

   i)   too concentrated.

   ....

   ii)   too dilute.

   ....

b)   He calculates that a patient taking part in the trial should take **250 ml** of a **0.2 M** solution of substance X each day. Describe how he could make up this strength solution.

   ....

   ....

Q6   'Screenwash' for cars is sold as an undiluted liquid for use all year round.

> **'Screenwash' Recommended Dilutions:**
> Normal use: 1 part screenwash to 4 parts water.
> Winter: 1 part screenwash to 2 parts water.
> Severe winter conditions: do not dilute.

a)   Suggest two reasons why the product is sold as the undiluted liquid and not diluted ready for use.

   1. ....

   2. ....

b)   What quantities of water and undiluted screenwash would you need to use to make up:

   i)   1000 ml (1 litre) of diluted screenwash for normal use.

   ....

   ii)   300 ml of diluted screenwash for winter use.

   ....

Q7   Heather needs to produce **200 cm³** of **0.1 M** hydrochloric acid solution for an experiment. She has been provided with a **2 M** hydrochloric acid solution and some water.

   Describe how Heather could make the required solution.

   ....

   ....

Concentration

Q8   'Froggart's' blackcurrant cordial is **diluted** before drinking.
Its contents are summarised on the label, as shown.

Froggart's blackcurrent cordial
Contains real fruit juice!
Dilute using 1 part cordial to 5 parts water.

100 ml diluted cordial contains:
30 mg vitamin C (50% RDA)
10.6 g sugar
Trace of sodium & protein
189 kJ energy

a)   **i)**   What do the letters RDA stand for?

....

ii)   What does the RDA tell you?

....

b)   **i)**   Donald pours a 10 ml serving of the cordial. How much water should he add?

....

ii)   What percentage of the RDA will this volume of cordial provide?

....

Work out the volume of diluted cordial first.

c)   What volume of diluted cordial would provide 100% of the RDA?

....

Q9   The **nutritional information** on the label of some vegetable stock powder is shown below.

	g per 100 g stock powder	g per 250 ml serving
protein	10.5	0.5
carbohydrate	29.4	1.5
fat	8.1	0.4
fibre	0.7	0.04
sodium	17.6	0.9

a)   150 g of powder will make 7.5 litres of stock. What volume will 100 g of powder make?

....

b)   Show that the mass of sodium given for a 250 ml serving agrees with that given for 100 g of powder.

....

....

c)   Sodium is present mainly as sodium chloride (salt).
How much sodium chloride will 100 g of stock powder contain?

....

....

d)   Suggest why this is probably an overestimate of the amount of salt in the stock powder.

....

Titrations

Q1   Label the following pieces of apparatus used in a titration experiment.

a) ....

b) ....

c) ....

d) ....

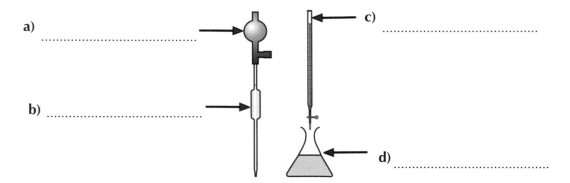

Q2   An **indicator** is used to determine the **end-point** of a titration.

a)   Complete the following table to show the colour of the indicators in different solutions.

Indicator	Colour in strong acid solutions	Colour in strong alkali solutions
phenolphthalein		
methyl orange		
litmus		

b)   Explain why universal indicator is **not** a suitable indicator to use in an acid-base titration.

....

....

Q3   Sophie wanted to find out the volume of an acidic solution required to neutralise 25 cm³ of an alkaline solution. She did a rough titration first, then four more titrations. Her results are shown in the table.

a)   Why did Sophie carry out a rough titration at the beginning?

....

....

b)   Which value is anomalous? ....

Titration	Volume of acid added / cm³
1	16.0
2	15.4
3	17.6
4	15.3
5	15.5

c)   What is the advantage of carrying out the titration several times?

....

d)   Calculate the average volume of acid needed to neutralise 25 cm³ of the alkaline solution.

....

More on Titrations

Q1 The graph shows the **pH curve** from a titration.

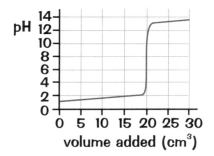

a) Write the general word equation for a neutralisation reaction.

....

b) Does this pH curve show an acid being added to an alkali or an alkali being added to an acid?

....

c) How is the end-point of a titration illustrated on a pH curve?

....

d) What volume of alkali is needed to neutralise the acid? ....

Q2 Anna carried out a titration in which **hydrochloric acid** was gradually added to **10 cm³** of calcium hydroxide solution in a conical flask. The results are shown in the table.

Volume of HCl (cm³)	pH
0	11.0
2	10.6
4	10.1
5	6.0
6	2.0
8	1.4
10	1.1

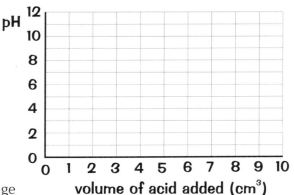

a) Plot a graph on the grid provided to show the change in pH as the titration proceeds. Draw a 'best fit' curve.

b) Estimate the pH after 7 cm³ of acid has been added. ....

c) What volume of acid was needed to neutralise the alkali? ....

Q3 **20 cm³ of a sodium hydroxide** solution was titrated with **0.1 M hydrochloric acid**. **10 cm³** of hydrochloric acid was needed to neutralise the alkali. Calculate the concentration of the sodium hydroxide solution using the steps below.

a) How many moles of hydrochloric acid were needed to neutralise the alkali?

....

b) How many moles of sodium hydroxide reacted? ....

c) Calculate the concentration of the sodium hydroxide. Give your answer in mol/dm³.

....

More on Titrations

Q4   Alex wanted to analyse the concentration of **phosphoric acid** in different brands of cola drinks. He allowed the carbon dioxide to escape from the drinks and titrated **20 cm³** of each drink using **0.01 M sodium hydroxide solution**. He used a pH meter to measure the pH.

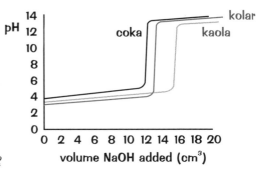

The results are shown in the graphs opposite.

a) Suggest why Alex used a pH meter instead of an indicator?

....

b) Suggest why Alex allowed the carbon dioxide to escape before analysing the drinks.

CO_2 in water gives carbonic acid.

....

c) Which drink had the greatest phosphoric acid concentration? ....

Q5   In a titration, **12.5 cm³** of **0.04 M calcium hydroxide** solution was needed to neutralise **25 cm³** of **sulfuric acid**. Calculate the **concentration** of the sulfuric acid in mol/dm³.

$$H_2SO_4 + Ca(OH)_2 \rightarrow CaSO_4 + 2H_2O$$

....

....

....

Q6   In a titration, **10 cm³** of **hydrochloric acid solution** was used to neutralise **30 cm³** of **0.1 mol/dm³ potassium hydroxide solution**.

$$HCl + KOH \rightarrow KCl + H_2O$$

What was the concentration of the hydrochloric acid in moles per dm³?

....

....

....

Top Tips:
Aargh, calculations. As if Chemistry wasn't tricky enough without maths getting involved too (but at least it's not as bad as Physics). Actually, these aren't the worst calculations as long as you tackle them in stages and know your equations.

Gas Volumes

Q1 Complete the sentences by circling one answer in each pair.

a) Gas syringes usually give **volumes** / **areas** of gas accurate to the nearest **dm³** / **cm³**.

b) A burette is **more** / **less** accurate for measuring the volume of gas collected than a measuring cylinder because the graduations on a burette are to the nearest **0.1 cm³** / **10 cm³**.

c) A balance can be used to measure the **volume** / **mass** of gas released in a reaction. The mass of the reactants **increases** / **decreases** as the reaction proceeds.

Q2 Choose the **most suitable method**, from A to D, for the tasks below. (Use each method once only.)

A — Bubble the gas into an upside-down gas jar filled with water.

B — Attach the conical flask to an empty boiling tube.

C — Bubble the gas into an upside-down burette filled with water.

D — Attach the conical flask to a gas syringe.

Sulfur dioxide and ammonia are soluble in water.

a) Collecting and measuring ammonia gas. ....

b) Collecting and measuring oxygen. ....

c) Collecting hydrogen. ....

d) Collecting sulfur dioxide. ....

Q3 a) What is the **volume** of **one mole** of any gas at room temperature and pressure? Circle your answer.

24 litres   **12 litres**   **2.4 litres**   **36 litres**

b) What volume is occupied by the following gases at room temperature and pressure?

i) 0.5 moles of hydrogen chloride. ....

ii) 6.25 moles of ammonia. ....

c) How many moles are there in the following gases at room temperature and pressure?

i) 240 cm³ of hydrogen. ....

ii) 8 dm³ of chlorine. ....

Q4 Look at the two sets of apparatus. Both were used to collect and measure a volume of **sulfur dioxide gas**. Exactly the same amount of sulfur dioxide was produced in each case and the temperature and pressure were identical.

A   **B**

Which set of apparatus do you think gave the more reliable results? Give an explanation for the difference.

....

....

Following Reactions

Q1 Use the words provided to complete the passage below.

new	gas	highest	faster	reaction	reactants	slower	limiting

You can tell that a chemical .... is taking place if a

.... substance is forming. You may see a colour change, a precipitate

forming or a .... being given off. Reactions are ....

at the start because this is when the reactants are at their ....

concentrations. Eventually the reaction gets ...., and it stops when one

of the .... is used up. This is called the .... reactant.

Q2 Tim adds a large piece of **magnesium** to some dilute **hydrochloric acid** and records the total volume of gas produced every 10 seconds. His results are shown in the graph below.

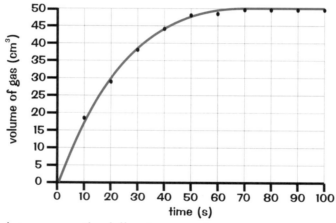

a) Use the graph to answer the following questions.

    i) How long did it take for the reaction to stop? ....

    ii) How much hydrogen was produced in total? ....

    iii) How much gas had been formed by 25 seconds? ....

    iv) How long did it take to produce 25 cm³ of hydrogen gas? ....

    At the end of the reaction Tim noticed that a very small piece of **magnesium** was left in the flask.

b) Which of the reactants is the limiting reactant?

....

c) Circle the correct answer to the following questions.

    i) If the amount of limiting reactant is halved, the total volume of hydrogen produced is:

        25 cm³   50 cm³   75 cm³   100 cm³

    ii) If the amount of limiting reactant is doubled, the total volume of hydrogen produced is:

        25 cm³   50 cm³   100 cm³   Not possible to predict.

Following Reactions

Q3 The graph shows the results of a reaction carried out under three different sets of **conditions**.

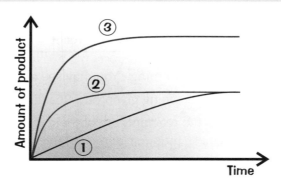

Match the following descriptions to the correct curve.

a) The reaction with the largest amount of limiting reactant.   ....

b) The reaction with the least amount of limiting reactant at the lowest temperature.   ....

c) The reaction with the least amount of limiting reactant at a higher temperature.   ....

Q4 The graph below shows the results of a reaction between **10 g** of **medium-sized marble chips** and **25 cm³** of **0.5 M hydrochloric acid**. (The acid is the limiting reactant.)

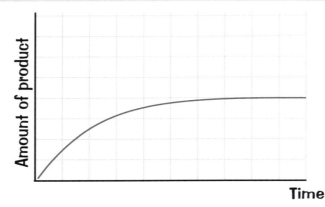

For each of the following reactions, sketch and label a curve of the reaction on the graph above and explain why you have drawn that particular curve.
(The acid is the limiting reactant in all the reactions.)

a) **Reaction 1** — 10 g of medium-sized marble chips with 25 cm³ of 1.0 M hydrochloric acid.

....

b) **Reaction 2** — 10 g of large marble chips with 25 cm³ of 0.5 M hydrochloric acid.

....

c) **Reaction 3** — 10 g of medium-sized marble chips with 12.5 cm³ of 1.0 M hydrochloric acid.

....

Top Tip: If you can't read graphs and tables, you'll struggle with questions about following reactions. Never fear though — all it takes is practice and you'll be an expert. Bored, but an expert.

Equilibrium

Q1   Use words from the list below to complete the following passage.

reversible	decrease	equilibrium	faster	increase	escape
reactants	closed	products	react	equal	slower

A reaction that can go in both directions is called a .... reaction. This means that the .... of the reaction can themselves .... to give the original .... To reach equilibrium, the reaction must happen in a .... system where products and reactants can't ....

As the reactants react their concentrations will ...., so the forward reaction will get .... At the same time, the concentration of the products will ...., which makes the backward reaction get ....
When the rates are ...., the reaction has reached an
....

Q2   Look at this diagram of a **reversible reaction**.

The reaction going from left to right is called the forward reaction. The reaction going from right to left is called the backward reaction.

a)   For the forward reaction:

   i)   Give the reactant(s). ....

   ii)   Give the product(s). ....

b)   **i)**   Here are two labels:

   | X   product splits up |
   | Y   reactants combine |

   Which of these labels
   goes in position 1 — X or Y? ....

   ii)   Which label goes in position 2 — X or Y? ....

c)   Write the equation for the reversible reaction. ....

Q3   The **position** of an **equilibrium** can be manipulated.

a)   Name three things that can change the position of an equilibrium.

....

b)   Why will a reversible reaction never reach equilibrium in an open beaker?

....

....

c)   Why doesn't the addition of a catalyst affect the amount of product formed?

....

....

Changing Equilibrium

Q1   Write the letter of one equation, A to C, to which the following statements apply.

A $N_2O_4(g) \rightleftharpoons 2NO_2(g)$

B $2SO_2(g) + O_2(g) \rightleftharpoons 2SO_3(g)$

C $H_2(g) + I_2(g) \rightleftharpoons 2HI(g)$

a)   A change in pressure has no effect on the position of equilibrium. ....

b)   An increase in pressure moves the equilibrium to the left. ....

c)   An increase in pressure moves the equilibrium to the right. ....

Q2   Substances A and B react to produce substances C and D in a reversible reaction.

$$2A(g) + B(g) \rightleftharpoons 2C(g) + D(g)$$

a)   The forward reaction is **exothermic**. Does the backward reaction give out or take in heat? Explain your answer.

....

....

b)   If the **temperature** is raised, will the forward or the backward reaction increase? ....

c)   Explain why changing the temperature of a reversible reaction always affects the position of equilibrium.

....

....

d)   What effect will changing the **pressure** have on the position of equilibrium of this reaction? Explain your answer.

....

Q3   The graph shows how the percentage of **ammonia** produced during the Haber process varies with the **conditions**.

a)   How does the % of ammonia produced change as the **pressure increases**?

....

b)   How does the % of ammonia produced change as the **temperature increases**?

....

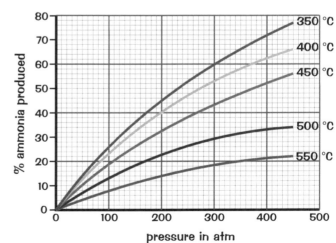

c)   Explain, using the data from the graph, whether the reaction is exothermic or endothermic.

....

....

Changing Equilibrium

Q4   **Ethanol** is produced from **ethene** and **steam**. The equation for the reaction is given below.

$$C_2H_4(g) + H_2O(g) \rightleftharpoons C_2H_5OH(g)$$

The table shows how the percentage of ethanol at equilibrium changes as the pressure changes (at a fixed temperature).

Pressure (atm)	20	30	40	50	60	70	80	90	100
% ethanol at equilibrium	20	24	28	32	38	43	48	54	59

a)   How many molecules are there on the left-hand side of the equation? ....

b)   What happens to the amount of **reactants** at equilibrium when the pressure is increased?

....

c)   Explain what happens to the percentage of ethanol at equilibrium when the pressure **decreases**.

....

....

Q5   For each of the following reactions, describe what would happen to the **position** of the equilibrium if the **temperature** and **pressure** of the mixture were **increased**.

a) $H_2(g) + Cl_2(g) \rightleftharpoons 2HCl(g)$ (forward reaction is exothermic)

Temperature ....

Pressure ....

b) $4NH_3(g) + 5O_2(g) \rightleftharpoons 4NO(g) + 6H_2O(g)$ (forward reaction is exothermic)

Temperature ....

Pressure ....

c) $N_2O_4(g) \rightleftharpoons 2NO_2(g)$ (forward reaction is endothermic)

Temperature ....

Pressure ....

d) $2SO_2(g) + O_2(g) \rightleftharpoons 2SO_3(g)$ (forward reaction is exothermic)

Temperature ....

Pressure ....

The Contact Process

Q1 Complete the following sentences by circling the correct word in each pair.

The **reduction** / **oxidation** of sulfur dioxide to sulfur trioxide is **exothermic** / **endothermic**.

When the temperature is increased, you get **more** / **less** sulfur trioxide, as the position of equilibrium is pushed to the **left** / **right**.

If the temperature of any reaction is increased, the rate of the reaction **decreases** / **increases** because the particles have **more** / **less** energy.

A high temperature gives a **high** / **low** yield of sulfur dioxide, but produces it **slowly** / **quickly**.

Q2 The graph shows the effect of **temperature** on the production of **sulfur trioxide**.

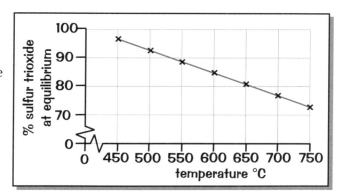

a) Describe how the percentage of sulfur trioxide at equilibrium changes with temperature.

....

....

....

b) At what temperature would you get 85% sulfur trioxide at equilibrium? ....

c) What percentage of sulfur trioxide would you get at 750 °C at equilibrium? ....

Q3 **Complete** and **balance** the following equations involved in the Contact Process.

a) $\quad$ .... $\;+\;$ .... $\;\rightarrow\; SO_2$

b) $\quad$ .... $\;+\;$ .... $\;\rightleftharpoons\;$ .... SO_3

c) $\quad SO_3 +$ .... $\;\rightarrow\;$ ....

Q4 The Contact Process uses **atmospheric pressure** to make sulfur trioxide.

a) Explain what happens to the yield of sulfur trioxide when the pressure is increased.

....

....

b) Give two reasons why the contact process is carried out at atmospheric pressure.

....

....

Strong and Weak Acids

Q1 Which of the following are strong acids? Circle your answer(s).

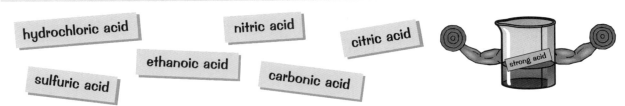

hydrochloric acid

nitric acid

citric acid

ethanoic acid

carbonic acid

sulfuric acid

strong acid

Q2 Tick the correct boxes to show whether the following statements are **true** or **false**.

		True	False
a)	Strong acids always have higher concentrations than weak acids.	☐	☐
b)	Strong acids ionise almost completely in water.	☐	☐
c)	Nitric acid ionises only very slightly in water.	☐	☐
d)	Weak acids ionise irreversibly in water.	☐	☐

Q3 Strong and weak acids react with **reactive metals** and with **carbonates** in the same way.

a) Complete the sentences by circling the correct word(s) in each pair.

   i) Hydrochloric acid and ethanoic acid react with magnesium to give **hydrogen / oxygen**.

   ii) Hydrochloric acid and ethanoic acid react with calcium carbonate to give
   carbon dioxide / carbon monoxide.

b) **i)** Do strong acids react **faster** or **slower** than weak acids? ....

   ii) Explain your answer. ....

   ....

   ....

Q4 The graph shows the results of a reaction between
0.1 mol of **magnesium** and **50 cm³** of **0.2 M**
hydrochloric acid. (The acid is the limiting reactant.)

For each of the following reactions, sketch a
curve on the graph above. (The acid is still
the limiting reactant in both reactions.)

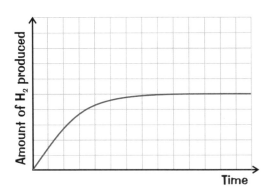

Amount of H₂ produced

Time

a) **Reaction 1** — 0.1 mol of magnesium is reacted with 50 cm³ of 0.4 mol/dm³ hydrochloric acid.

b) **Reaction 2** — 0.1 mol of magnesium is reacted with 50 cm³ of 0.2 mol/dm³ ethanoic acid.

Top Tip: Strong and weak acids are similar but different, and it's all down to how much they
ionise. If you know that weak acids only ionise a bit, all the rest pretty much follows on from there.

Strong and Weak Acids

Q5 Write **equations** to show the **ionisation** of the following acids.

a) Hydrochloric acid (HCl) ....

b) Ethanoic acid (CH₃COOH) ....

Q6 Fred has been asked to design an experiment to show that hydrochloric acid reacts faster than ethanoic acid with **magnesium ribbon**.

a) Give two variables that should be kept constant to make it a fair experiment.

1. ....

2. ....

b) Suggest how Fred could collect and measure the gas.

....

c) What difference would you expect to see in the amount of gas collected after:

i) both acids had reacted for 20 seconds?

....

ii) both acids had reacted completely?

....

Q7 Explain the following:

a) The pH of nitric acid is lower than the pH of lactic acid (of the same concentrations).

....

....

b) Hydrochloric acid is a better electrical conductor than carbonic acid (of the same concentration).

....

....

c) Weak acids and strong acids of the same concentration will produce the same amount of product.

....

....

d) Weak acids are used as descalers.

....

....

122

Precipitation Reactions

Q1 Look at the **equations** below, then complete the sentences by circling one answer in each pair.

> barium nitrate + potassium sulfate $\rightleftharpoons$ barium sulfate + potassium nitrate
> $Ba(NO_3)_2(aq)$ + $K_2SO_4(aq)$ $\rightleftharpoons$ $BaSO_4(s)$ + $2KNO_3(aq)$

a) The precipitate formed is **BaSO₄** / **KNO₃**. This is shown by the state symbol **aq** / **s**.

b) The **potassium** / **barium** ions are called spectator ions, they're not involved in the reaction.

c) The ionic equation only involves the ions that **remain in solution** / **precipitate out**.

d) The reaction is **fast** / **slow**.

Q2 Deirdre wants to find out if a soluble compound contains **chloride**, **bromide** or **iodide** ions.

a) Describe how she could do this.

....

....

b) Match the **compounds** on the left to the correct **test result** on the right.

KCl (aq)   a yellow precipitate

NaI (aq)   a cream precipitate

CaBr₂ (aq)   a white precipitate

Q3 Jason has been given a solid sample which he suspects is **magnesium sulfate** ($MgSO_4$).

a) Describe a method Jason could use to show that the compound contains sulfate ions.

....

....

b) What is the positive result of the test described in part a)?

....

c) Write an ionic equation for this reaction (remember to include state symbols).

....

Q4 Explain why **ionic substances** in precipitation reactions must be **in solution**.

....

....

Module C5 — How Much?

Preparing Insoluble Salts

Q1   **Lead(II) nitrate** was reacted with **sodium iodide** to give an insoluble salt.

a)   Which of the following is the correctly balanced symbol equation for this reaction? Tick one box.

   A $PbNO_3(aq) + NaI(aq) \rightarrow PbI_2(aq) + 2NaNO_3(aq)$ ☐

   B $Pb(NO_3)_2(aq) + 2NaI(aq) \rightarrow PbI_2(s) + 2NaNO_3(aq)$ ☐

   C $Pb(NO_3)_2(aq) + 2NaI(s) \rightarrow PbI_2(aq) + 2NaNO_3(s)$ ☐

b)   Name the **insoluble salt** formed. ....

Q2   Complete the following equations, then write the **ionic** equation for each reaction.

Remember to include state symbols.

a) $Pb(NO_3)_2(aq) + 2NaCl(aq) \rightarrow$ .... $+ 2NaNO_3(aq)$

   Ionic equation: ....

b) $MgSO_4(aq) + BaCl_2(aq) \rightarrow$ .... $+ MgCl_2(aq)$

   Ionic equation: ....

c) $NH_4Cl(aq) + AgNO_3(aq) \rightarrow$ .... $+ NH_4NO_3(aq)$

   Ionic equation: ....

d) $Pb(NO_3)_2(aq) + ZnSO_4(aq) \rightarrow$ .... $+ Zn(NO_3)_2(aq)$

   Ionic equation: ....

Q3   Louise wants to prepare the insoluble salt **barium sulfate**. She starts by making two solutions, one of barium nitrate and one of copper(II) sulfate.

a)   What should Louise check before she handles any of the chemicals?

   ....

b)   Louise uses tap water to dissolve the solids. What would be a better choice, and why?

   ....

c)   Write the balanced symbol equation for this reaction.

   ....

d)   Outline the rest of the method she should use.

   ....

   ....

Mixed Questions — Module C5

Q1 There are two common oxides of chromium, **oxide V** and **oxide W**.

a) 5.2 g of chromium reacted with 2.4 g of oxygen to produce oxide V.
Calculate the empirical formula of oxide V.

....

b) Oxide W has a percentage composition by mass of 52% chromium and 48% oxygen.
Work out its empirical formula.

....

Q2 During the contact process, **sulfur dioxide** reacts with **oxygen** to form **sulfur trioxide**.

a) Write down the balanced symbol equation for this reaction.

....

b) What catalyst is used most often in this reaction? ....

c) i) Is this reaction exothermic or endothermic? ....

ii) Would high or low temperatures favour a high rate of reaction? ....

d) i) How many moles of reactant react to produce two moles of product? ....

ii) Would high or low pressures favour a high yield of product? ....

e) i) What are the actual industrial conditions used during the production of sulfur trioxide?

....

ii) Why are these a compromise? ....

....

Q3 Simon wants to know if an unknown compound contains a **halogen**.

a) Describe a test that Simon could do to show if halide ions are present.

....

....

b) The test gives a cream precipitate.

i) Which halide ion is present? ....

ii) Write an ionic equation for the reaction. ....

c) Describe how Simon could get a dry sample of the precipitate.

....

....

Mixed Questions — Module C5

Q4 During a reaction, **0.12 g** of **magnesium** reacts completely with **20 cm³** of **nitric acid** to form **magnesium nitrate** and **hydrogen**. The acid is neutralised exactly.

$$Mg_{(s)} + 2HNO_{3(aq)} \rightarrow Mg(NO_3)_{2(aq)} + H_{2(g)}$$

a) Calculate the number of moles of magnesium used.

....

b) Calculate the concentration of nitric acid used in mol/dm³.

....

c) **i)** Work out the relative formula mass of magnesium nitrate.

....

ii) Work out the mass of magnesium nitrate produced.

....

d) Calculate the volume of hydrogen gas formed (at RTP).

....

Q5 Brenda wants to find out the concentration of a solution of sodium hydroxide. She carries out a **titration** using **15 cm³** of **0.2 M** hydrochloric acid, and finds that it takes **22 cm³** of sodium hydroxide to neutralise the acid.

a) Brenda only has **2 M** hydrochloric acid.

Describe how she could make 100 cm³ of the required strength solution.

....

....

b) Calculate the concentration of the sodium hydroxide solution, in **mol/dm³**.

....

....

....

c) Calculate the concentration of the sodium hydroxide solution, in **g/dm³**.

....

....

Mixed Questions — Module C5

Q6 The graph opposite shows the reactions between **calcium carbonate** and two different **acids**. The reactions were carried out using identical conditions, and the same concentration and volumes of acid.

a) Name the gas produced in both reactions.

....

b) Which line shows the faster reaction? ....

c) The acids are **ethanoic acid** and **sulfuric acid**. Which line shows the reaction between **sulfuric acid** and calcium carbonate? Explain your answer.

....

....

d) Which acid would be more useful as a **descaling agent** for a kettle? Explain your answer.

....

....

Q7 The diagram opposite shows the electrolysis of **copper(II) sulfate solution**, with copper electrodes.

a) Complete the half-equations for the reaction at each electrode.

i) At the positive electrode:

$$Cu \rightarrow \text{...............} + \text{................}$$

ii) At the negative electrode:

$$Cu^{2+} + \text{................} \rightarrow \text{................}$$

b) **i)** Calculate the mass of copper formed at the negative electrode, if 2 amps flows through the solution of copper(II) sulfate for 30 minutes.

....

....

....

....

....

ii) What mass of copper was lost from the positive electrode? ....

Redox and Displacement Reactions

Q1 Imagine that four new metals, **antium**, **bodium**, **candium** and **dekium** have recently been discovered. Bodium displaces antium but not candium or dekium. Dekium displaces all the others. Put the new metals into their order of reactivity, from the most to the least reactive.

most reactive ....

....

....

least reactive ....

"Ahaarr... buried antium."

Q2 Match each term to its correct description.

reduction   loss of electrons

oxidising agent   gain of electrons

oxidation   a chemical that accepts electrons and becomes reduced

reducing agent   a chemical that donates electrons and becomes oxidised

Q3 A piece of **magnesium** is dropped into blue **copper(II) sulfate** ($CuSO_4$) solution.

a) What are the products of the resulting reaction?

....

Magnesium is a more reactive metal than copper.

b) Are the magnesium atoms **oxidised** or **reduced** in this reaction?

....

c) Write a **balanced** symbol equation (including state symbols) for this reaction.

....

Q4 Zinc reacts with iron(II) sulfate solution in a **redox reaction**.

a) What is a 'redox reaction'?

....

b) Which metal is becoming:

i) oxidised? ....   ii) reduced? ....

c) Write balanced half-equations for the:

i) oxidation reaction ....

Make sure the charges balance — they should be the same on both sides of the arrow.

ii) reduction reaction ....

Redox and Displacement Reactions

Q5   **Titanium** is extracted from its chloride, **TiCl$_4$**, by reaction with **magnesium**.

a)   Write the balanced symbol equation for this reaction.

....

b)   During this reaction, which metal:

i)   loses electrons?   ....

ii)   is reduced?   ....

iii)   is acting as a reducing agent?   ....

Please Note:
Due to printing restriction, a "Red Ox"
could not be shown on this page.
Please be amused by this blue goat instead.

Q6   Graham added equal amounts of **magnesium powder** into test tubes containing solutions of equal concentrations of either **calcium**, **iron** or **zinc chloride**. The **temperature** of each was measured before and after any reaction.

Solution	Temp. at start (°C)	Temp. at end (°C)	Temp. change (°C)
CaCl$_2$	20	20	
ZnCl$_2$	21	24	
FeCl$_2$	19	24	

a)   Complete the table by calculating the temperature change for each solution.

b)   Is the reaction between magnesium and iron chloride **exothermic** or **endothermic**?

....

c)   Why was there **no** temperature rise with the calcium chloride solution?

....

d)   Use these results to put magnesium, calcium, iron and zinc in a **reactivity series**.

most reactive   ....

....

....

least reactive   ....

e)   Which of these metals is the strongest **oxidising agent**? Explain your answer.

....

f)   What could Graham do to improve the **accuracy** of his results?

....

Rusting of Iron

Q1 Paul carries out an experiment to investigate **rusting**. He puts
three **iron** nails into separate test tubes, as shown in the diagram.

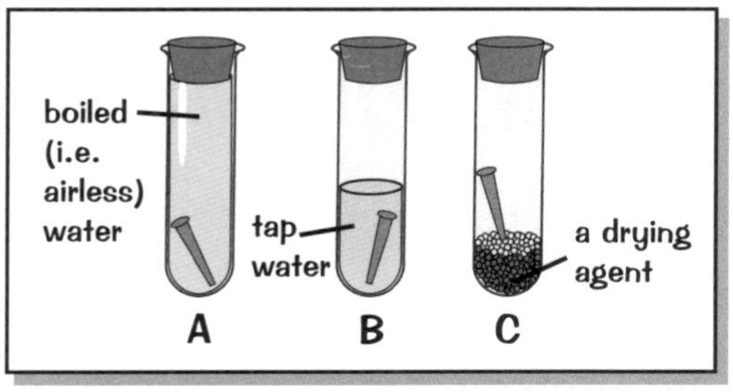

a) What **two** things are needed for iron to rust?

....

boiled
(i.e.
airless)
water

tap
water

a drying
agent

A   B   C

b) In which of these tubes will the iron rust most quickly?

....

c) Write a **word equation** for the formation of rust.

....

Q2 Circle the correct words from each pair below.

Iron **loses** / **gains** electrons when it reacts with oxygen. The **oxygen** / **iron** is oxidised in

the reaction. Each **oxygen** / **iron** atom loses **three** / **two** electrons to give O^{2-} / Fe^{3+}.

Q3 Tick the boxes to show whether each of the following statements is **true** or **false**.

True False

a) Stainless steel is a rustproof alloy of iron, steel and chromium. ☐ ☐

b) Painting metal items prevents them rusting by keeping out oxygen and water. ☐ ☐

c) Rusting is a redox reaction ☐ ☐

d) Sacrificial protection involves a displacement reaction. ☐ ☐

Q4 Iron pipes can be protected from rusting by having **magnesium** bars attached to them.

a) Explain why this type of protection is known as 'the **sacrificial** method'.

....

b) Explain why copper cannot be used to protect iron pipes.

....

c) Explain what galvanising is, and how it prevents iron from rusting.

....

....

Q5 Iron is sometimes coated with tin to prevent it from rusting.

Explain why this method doesn't prevent rusting if the tin is scratched.

....

....

Fuel Cells

Q1   **Hydrogen** and **oxygen** react together in an **exothermic** reaction.

a)   What is the **only** product when hydrogen and oxygen react together? ....

b)   What is an exothermic reaction?

....

c)   Sketch an energy level diagram to show the above reaction.

Q2   Fill in the blanks to complete the passage below.

A fuel cell is an electrical cell that's supplied with a ....
and .... and uses energy from the reaction between
them to generate a ....

Q3   The diagram shows a hydrogen-oxygen **fuel cell**.

a)   What goes into the cell at A and B?

A .... B ....

b)   What comes out of the cell at C?

....

c)   What could the electrodes be made of?

....

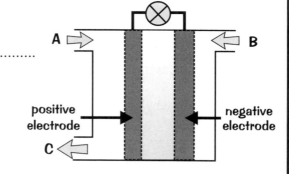

d)   What could be used as the electrolyte? ....

e)   Write the symbol equation for the reaction that occurs at the:

i)   negative electrode. ....

ii) positive electrode. ....

f)   Write the overall equation for the reaction in the cell. ....

Fuel Cells

Q4 Draw lines to connect the two halves of these sentences about **hydrogen-oxygen fuel cells**.

Fuel cells are more efficient than...   ...so there is no harmful pollution.

In a fuel cell electricity is generated...   ...batteries or power stations.

Fuel cells waste less heat energy...   ...so no energy is lost due to friction.

Fuel cells have no moving parts...   ...directly from the reaction.

Fuel cells produce only water...   ...as they use fewer stages.

Q5 Complete this table comparing different ways of **generating electricity**.

Method	'Fuel'	Portable? (Yes/No)	Pollutants released	Efficiency (High/Low)
Coal-fired power station			gases, e.g. CO_2, CO, SO_2 etc.	
Battery	chemicals			
Hydrogen fuel cell				

Q6 Give three advantages of using hydrogen fuel cells on **spacecraft**.

1. ....

2. ....

3. ....

Q7 **Cars** are being developed that run on fuel cells.

a) Explain how using these cars could help reduce the amount of air pollution in cities.

....

....

b) Name **two** other possible uses of fuel cells.

....

Q8 Explain why hydrogen fuel cells are unlikely to end of our dependence on fossil fuels.

....

....

Alcohols

Q1 **Alcohols** are a common group of chemicals.

a) What is the general formula of an alcohol? ....

b) Complete the following table.

Alcohol	No. Carbon Atoms	Molecular Formula	Displayed Formula
Methanol			
	2		
		C_3H_7OH	
			H H H H │ │ │ │ H–C–C–C–C–O–H │ │ │ │ H H H H
	5		

Q2 The molecular formula for **ethanol** can be written as C_2H_5OH or as C_2H_6O.

a) What is the functional group found in all alcohols? ....

b) Explain why it is better to write ethanol's formula as C_2H_5OH.

....

Q3 Ethanol can be dehydrated to make ethene.

a) Name two sections of the chemical industry that use ethene.

....

b) Write a symbol equation for the conversion of ethanol into ethene.

....

c) What could be used as a catalyst for this process?

....

Top Tips: You may be surprised to hear that the main use of ethanol is as a **motor fuel** and **fuel additive** — not in alcoholic drinks as I previously thought. It's also used as a solvent and an antiseptic.

Module C6 — Chemistry Out There

Alcohols

Q4 Choose from the words in the box to fill in the gaps in the passage below about fermentation.

concentration	10–20%	25 °C	35 °C	50 °C	30–40%	temperature
oxygen	hot	cold	sugars	enzymes	ethanoic acid	

Fermentation is used to turn .... into ethanol. The reaction happens

due to .... found in yeasts. The .... needs to be

carefully controlled during the reaction — if it is too .... the reaction is

very slow, and if it is too .... the .... are destroyed.

The optimum is between .... and ....

It is important to stop .... getting into the reaction mixture, because it

converts the ethanol to ....

The reaction stops when the .... of the ethanol reaches

about ...., because the yeast are killed by the alcohol.

Q5 There are **two** ways of making **ethanol**:

A sugar → ethanol + carbon dioxide + energy   **B** ethene + steam → ethanol

a) Which of the word equations describes making ethanol by the fermentation method? ....

b) Give a balanced symbol equation for each of the reactions shown above.

A ....

B ....

c) Ethanol can be used as a fuel. In some countries the fermentation method is often used to produce it. Give two reasons why this method is chosen.

1. ....

2. ....

d) Describe a **disadvantage** of the fermentation method.

....

e) What conditions are needed to make ethanol from ethene and steam?

....

....

Salt

Q1   Indicate whether the following statements about obtaining salt are **true** or **false**.

		True	False
a)	In the UK most salt is obtained by evaporation in flat open tanks.	☐	☐
b)	There are massive deposits of rock salt in the Lake District and Kent.	☐	☐
c)	Salt can be mined by pumping hot water underground.	☐	☐
d)	Some holes left by mining salt must be filled in, or they could cause subsidence.	☐	☐

Q2   Describe three ways that **rock salt** is used.

1. ....

2. ....

3. ....

Q3   **Circle** the correct answer for each of the questions below.

a)   One of the products of the electrolysis of brine is chlorine. You can test for it by:

Using a glowing splint — chlorine will relight it.

Using damp litmus paper — chlorine will bleach it.

Using universal indicator — chlorine will turn it purple.

b)   Two of the products of electrolysis are reacted together to make household bleach. They are:

Chlorine and hydrogen.   Chlorine and sodium hydroxide.

Hydrogen and sodium hydroxide.

Q4   The diagram shows the **industrial set-up** used to electrolyse concentrated brine.

a)   Identify the substances labelled A, B, C and D on the diagram. Choose from the options in the box below.

Na	O$_2$	Cl$_2$	H$_2$
brine	NaOH	H$_2$O	

A ....   B ....

C ....   D ....

b)   Write **balanced** half-equations for the reactions that occur during the electrolysis of this salt solution.

Anode: ....

Cathode: ....

Make sure the charges balance.

c)   Why are inert electrodes used?

....

Module C6 — Chemistry Out There

Salt

Q5 Harry runs a little **brine electrolysis** business from his garden shed. He keeps a record of all the different **industries** that he sells his products to.

HARRY'S BRINE PRODUCTS LTD. — FINAL USES

ceramics 2%
other 11%
disinfectants 8%
soap x%
plastics 21%
paper pulp 8%
insecticide
other 5%
other 11%
margarine 14%

- chlorine
- hydrogen
- sodium hydroxide

a) Which brine product, **hydrogen**, **chlorine** or **sodium hydroxide**, does Harry sell the most of?

....

b) What percentage of Harry's products are used to manufacture **soap**?

....

c) Which **industry** uses the biggest proportion of Harry's products? ....

Q6 When either **dilute** brine or **molten** sodium chloride are electrolysed, the products are different to those made from **concentrated** brine.

a) Complete the table to show what products are formed at each electrode.

	Product formed at:	
	Anode	Cathode
concentrated brine	chlorine	hydrogen
dilute brine		
molten sodium chloride		

b) Write the equations for the reactions happening at the electrodes with **dilute brine**.

Anode: .... Cathode: ....

c) Why are the reactions at the electrodes different with **dilute** brine than with concentrated brine?

....

....

d) Write the equations for the reactions happening at the electrodes with **molten sodium chloride**.

Anode: .... Cathode: ....

Top Tips: Well, I bet you really didn't want to know that much about salt. In fact, I reckon you would have been happy just knowing that you can put it on your chips. But unfortunately, you're going to have to know all of its industrial uses AND what products you get when you electrolyse concentrated brine, dilute brine and molten sodium chloride. It's tough, but someone's got to do it.

136

CFCs and the Ozone Layer

Q1   CFCs are a **useful** group of chemicals.

a)   Which of the following shows the structure of a CFC? Circle your answer.

$$F-\underset{\underset{H}{|}}{\overset{\overset{Cl}{|}}{C}}-H \qquad F-\underset{\underset{F}{|}}{\overset{\overset{H}{|}}{C}}-F \qquad F-\underset{\underset{Cl}{|}}{\overset{\overset{Cl}{|}}{C}}-F \qquad H-\underset{\underset{Cl}{|}}{\overset{\overset{Cl}{|}}{C}}-H$$

b)   Which of the following are useful properties of CFCs? Circle your answer(s).

| non-flammable | soluble in water | high boiling point | non-toxic |

c)   Give **two** uses of CFCs.

....

Q2   Say whether the following statements about **ozone** are true or false.

		True	False
a)	Ozone is a form of oxygen with the formula O_3.	☐	☐
b)	Most ozone is found in the lower part of the Earth's atmosphere.	☐	☐
c)	Ozone does the important job of absorbing infrared light from the Sun.	☐	☐
d)	When ozone absorbs the Sun's energy, it breaks down into an oxygen molecule and an oxygen atom.	☐	☐

Q3   CFCs affect the ozone in the Earth's atmosphere.

a)   What effect do **CFCs** have on **ozone**?

....

b)   Describe how scientists became aware of this.

....

....

....

Q4   The thinning of the ozone layer is **dangerous**.

a)   How does the thinning of the ozone layer affect the amount of UV radiation reaching the Earth?

....

b)   Give three medical problems associated with this problem.

1. ....

2. ....

3. ....

Module C6 — Chemistry Out There

CFCs and the Ozone Layer

Q5 Choose from the words in the box to fill in the gaps in the passage below.

stratosphere	ions	infrared	thousands	unreactive
reactive	free radicals	one	troposphere	ultraviolet

CFCs are .... However, in the ....
where there is lots of high-energy .... light, they break up
to form .... Each CFC molecule produces one or more
chlorine atoms which can react with .... of ozone
molecules.

Q6 **Replacements** for CFCs are being developed.

a) Circle two substances from the list below that are thought to be suitable replacements for CFCs.

chlorocarbons   alkanes   trichlorides   alkenes   hydrofluorocarbons

b) One of the substances in the above list is a group of compounds that are very similar to CFCs. What is the important difference that makes these compounds safe to use?

....

Q7 **Free radicals** are very reactive particles.

a) Draw a dot and cross diagram in the box to show the covalent bond between the two hydrogen atoms in a hydrogen molecule.

b) What type of particle is formed when a covalent bond breaks:

i) unevenly (i.e. both electrons go to the same atom)?

....

ii) evenly (i.e. one electron goes to each atom)?

....

c) Give the symbol for a hydrogen free radical. ....

d) What makes free radicals so reactive? ....

Module C6 — Chemistry Out There

CFCs and the Ozone Layer

Q8 CFCs damage the ozone layer.

a) What causes CFCs to break up in the upper atmosphere?

....

b) Write an equation to show what happens to CCl_2F_2 when UV light hits it.

....

c) Describe why scientists originally thought that CFCs were safe to use.

....

....

....

Q9 **Free radicals** found in the upper atmosphere are responsible for the depletion of the ozone layer.

a) Write an equation to show what happens when a chlorine free radical hits an ozone molecule.

....

b) The chlorine oxide ($ClO\bullet$) free radical produced will then react with another ozone molecule. Write an equation to show this reaction.

....

c) How many ozone molecules are destroyed in these two reactions? ....

Q10 It's now clear that it was a mistake to use CFCs without fully understanding the effects they could have. Many countries have now **banned** the use of CFCs.

a) Why haven't **all** countries banned them?

....

b) Explain why the effects of CFCs are a global problem.

....

c) Explain why even a complete ban will not stop the damage to the ozone layer.

....

....

Top Tips: CFCs were ideal for many uses — the trouble was, we didn't fully understand what wider effects they would have. Now we're left with loads of CFCs in our upper atmosphere, and we can't do much about it.

Hardness of Water

Q1 Tick the correct boxes to show whether the statements are **true** or **false**.

True False

a) Rainwater which passes over limestone and chalk rocks becomes hard. ☐ ☐

b) Water can be softened by removing chloride and carbonate ions from the water. ☐ ☐

c) Adding sodium chloride is one way of removing hardness from water. ☐ ☐

d) Scale is formed when soap is used with hard water. ☐ ☐

e) You can remove the hardness from water by adding sodium carbonate. ☐ ☐

Q2 An **ion exchange column** can be used to remove the hardness from water.

a) Explain how hard water becomes soft when it is passed through an **ion exchange column**.

....

....

b) Does this method work for permanent hardness, temporary hardness, or both?

....

Q3 Angelica's kettle has become **scaled up**, and it takes ages to make a cup of tea (it's really getting on her nerves).

a) Why does the limescale in Angelica's kettle mean that her cup of tea takes longer to prepare?

....

b) She buys a descaling product to sort out the tea problem.
Which of the following would you expect it to contain? Circle your answer.

a weak alkali   **a weak acid**   **a strong alkali**   **a strong acid**

c) Explain why the substance you have chosen makes a good descaler.

....

....

Q4 **Minerals** dissolve in water as it flows over rocks and through soil.

a) What two ions are responsible for causing hard water? ....

b) Calcium carbonate is found in many different types of rock. Name three of them.

....

c) Calcium carbonate rocks will not dissolve in pure water. How do these ions get into water?

....

....

Hardness of Water

Q5 A teacher wanted to demonstrate how chalk (composed of $CaCO_3$) dissolves in rainwater to produce **hard water**, and how it forms **scale** when it is boiled. She carried out the following experiments.

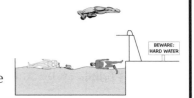

a) A spatula measure of powdered calcium carbonate was added to some distilled water and stirred. Why didn't the water become hard?

....

b) Carbon dioxide was bubbled through the mixture of calcium carbonate and distilled water.

i) Complete the equation below to show the reaction that took place.

$$CO_2(g) \ + \ H_2O(l) \ + \ CaCO_3(s) \ \rightarrow \ \text{.................(aq)}$$

ii) Why did the water become hard?

....

c) A solution of calcium hydrogencarbonate was boiled in a beaker. A white precipitate formed.

$$Ca(HCO_3)_2(aq) \ \rightarrow \ CaCO_3(s) \ + \ H_2O(l) \ + \ CO_2(g)$$

i) Name the white precipitate formed. ....

ii) Describe the problems this reaction can cause when it happens in **hot water pipes**.

....

....

Q6 In an experiment to investigate the **causes** of **hardness** in water, soap solution was added to different solutions. Five drops were added at a time until a sustainable lather was formed.

Solution	Drops of soap solution needed to produce a lather	Observations	Drops of detergent solution needed to produce a lather
distilled water	5	no scum	5
magnesium sulfate solution	35	scum formed	5
calcium chloride solution	30	scum formed	5
sodium chloride solution	5	no scum	5

a) Why must all the solutions be prepared from distilled water rather than tap water?

....

b) **i)** Which compounds caused hardness in the water? ....

ii) Explain how you know. ....

c) What role did the test using distilled water play in the experiment?

....

Top Tips: Hard water isn't very exciting, but at least it's not, well, hard. The only bits that will take some learning are the equations, especially that rather nasty calcium hydrogencarbonate one.

Fats and Oils

Q1   Fats and oils come from **plants** and **animals**.

a)   Name two fats or oils that come from plants and two that come from animals.

Plants: .... and ....

Animals: .... and ....

b)   Give two uses of natural fats and oils.

....

c)   What other raw material can be used to manufacture similar products?

....

Q2   Complete the passage below using some of the words in the box.

alcohols	fatty	strong	solids	acids	chubby
glycerol	esters	liquids	ethanol	gases	alkenes

Fats are .... at room temperature and oils are

.... Fats and oils are members of a group of chemicals

called .... These chemicals can be made by reacting

together .... and .... Hydrolysis breaks

up fats and oils into .... acids and ....

Q3   Butter and milk are **emulsions** of oil and water.

a)   Oil and water are **immiscible** — what does this mean?

....

b)   Describe what an emulsion is, and how to make one.

....

....

c)   Look at the diagrams below. Label the droplets of **oil** and the droplets of **water**.

droplets of ....   droplets of ....

milk   butter

Fats and Oils

Q4   Vegetable oils can be turned into **fuels**.

a)   Name two vegetable oils that can be turned into fuels.

.... and ....

b)   Why are vegetable oils suitable for processing into fuels?

....

c)   Suggest why fuels made from vegetable oils are environmentally friendly.

....

Q5   **Biodiesel** is a fuel made from vegetable oil. A litre of biodiesel contains **90%** of the energy in a litre of normal diesel.

a)   Normal diesel contains 37 MJ (37 000 000 J) of energy per litre. How much energy does a litre of biodiesel contain?

....

b)   Why can biodiesel be used as an alternative to diesel fuel?

....

Q6   Oils and fats can be used to make **soap**.

a)   What is saponification?

....

b)   Draw lines to connect the two parts of the following sentences.

Soap is made by...   ...boiling oil or fat with alkali.

The alkali usually used is...   ...glycerol is produced.

As well as soap...   ...sodium hydroxide.

c)   Write the word equation for making soap.

....

Top Tips: Fats are horrible. Like when you get a nice shoulder of lamb, but you can't eat half of it because it's all fat. And then you go and learn that when you're using soap, you're kind of washing your hands with fat. Ugghh. On second thoughts, I don't think anything could beat some butter spread thickly over some freshly baked bread... ummm...

Using Plant Oils

Q1   Ben and Martin both planned an experiment to identify saturated and unsaturated oils.

> **Ben's Method**
> 1. Put some oil in a test tube.
> 2. Add some bromine water.
> 3. Shake vigorously.
> 4. Repeat for next oil.
> 5. When all the oils are done, write down the results.

> **Martin's Method**
> 1. Put 2 ml of oil into a test tube.
> 2. Label the test tube with the name of the oil sample.
> 3. Add 5 drops of bromine water and shake.
> 4. Record any colour change.
> 5. Repeat for each oil.

Whose experimental method is better? Give reasons for your answer.

....

....

Q2   Match each label below to a fatty acid structure.

Saturated animal fat

Polyunsaturated grape seed oil

Monounsaturated olive oil

Q3   Margarine is usually made from partially hydrogenated vegetable oil.

a)   Describe how hydrogenation is carried out.

....

....

b)   How does hydrogenation affect the melting points of vegetable oils?

....

Q4   Some types of fats are considered bad for your heart.

a)   Explain why saturated fats are bad for your heart.

....

....

b)   Partially hydrogenated vegetable oil contains **trans fats**. What effect do these have on the blood?

....

....

Drugs

Q1 **Aspirin** is a drug used to reduce pain.

a) What is a drug?

....

b) What is the name given to drugs used to reduce pain? ....

c) Why must drugs be made from very pure chemicals?

....

Q2 Drugs can be extremely **dangerous** if an overdose is taken.

a) Which of the following is **not** a possible danger of an aspirin overdose? Circle your answer.

breathing problems   nausea   raised heart rate

internal bleeding   swelling

b) What is the main effect on the body of an overdose of paracetamol?

....

Q3 Here are the **displayed formulas** of aspirin, paracetamol and ibuprofen.

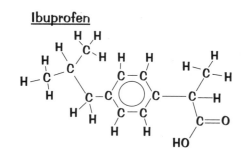

a) Give the molecular formula of each of these drugs.

aspirin ....   paracetamol ....   ibuprofen ....

b) Circle a structure on the diagram above that all three drugs have in common.

c) Which of the above drugs contain a $-COCH_3$ group?

....

d) Give two ways that the structure of paracetamol is different to the other two molecules.

....

Top Tips: The word 'analgesic' comes from two Greek words, 'an' meaning 'without' and 'algia' meaning 'pain' — but remember taking an overdose leads to horrendous amounts of pain.

Aspirin

Q1   Circle the correct words in each pair below to complete the passage about the **discovery** of aspirin.

> The leaves and bark of **birch / willow** trees have been used to ease pain for 2500 years. The active
> ingredient was isolated in 1828 and named **salicylic / acetylsalicylic** acid. However, this
> substance had side effects such as **mouth ulcers / liver damage**. Eventually, in 1897, scientists
> found a way to convert it into **salicylic / acetylsalicylic** acid, which we know as aspirin.

Q2   Aspirin is manufactured from **salicylic acid**.

a)   Write numbers in the boxes to put these steps in order and show how aspirin can be **synthesised**.

☐ The mixture is cooled and aspirin precipitates out.

☐ Add a few drops of concentrated sulfuric acid.

☐ The aspirin is filtered out and crystallised.

☐ Mix salicylic acid with ethanoic anhydride.

☐ Heat the mixture to 50 °C for a few minutes.

b)   Describe the industrial conditions used in producing aspirin.

....

....

Q3   Aspirin is a very widely used drug.

a)   Describe two beneficial effects of taking aspirin.

....

b)   Give two problems associated with taking aspirin.

....

....

Q4   The diagram shows the structure of **soluble** aspirin.

a)   On the diagram, circle the group that isn't present in ordinary aspirin.

b)   Why is ordinary aspirin insoluble?

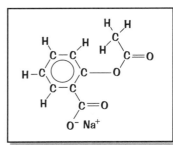

....

....

c)   Give an advantage of using soluble aspirin rather than ordinary aspirin.

....

Mixed Questions — Module C6

Q1   The products made by **electrolysing brine** have many uses.

a)   Look at the **uses** below and place each one into the correct box to show which **product** it requires.

PVC   soap   oven cleaner   margarine   water purification   disinfectant   ammonia   paper

CHLORINE	HYDROGEN	SODIUM HYDROXIDE

b)   i)   What is produced at the anode during the electrolysis of dilute brine? ....

ii)   Write a balanced symbol equation for this reaction.

....

Q2   **Hydrogen-oxygen fuel cells** involve a **redox reaction**.

a)   Give the half-equation at the **anode**. ....

b)   Give the half-equation at the **cathode**. ....

c)   Explain why the reaction is classed as a **redox reaction**.

....

....

d)   Give an example of a **use** for hydrogen fuel cells. ....

e)   Give two **advantages** of using hydrogen fuel cells compared to batteries.

1. ....

2. ....

Q3   The Forth Rail Bridge is the second longest three-cantilever rail bridge in the world. It is made of 54 000 tonnes of **steel** and is 2.5 km long.

The bridge has to be regularly **repainted**.

a)   Why was it necessary to constantly paint the bridge?

....

b)   Another type of steel is used for cutlery, but this is not painted. Explain why.

....

....

Module C6 — Chemistry Out There

Mixed Questions — Module C6

Q4   Aspirin is a commonly used **analgesic**.

a)   What is an analgesic? ....

b)   Name **two** other analgesics. ....

c)   In the old days, bark from a type of willow tree was used as a painkiller.

    i)   What chemical in the willow bark was responsible for the painkilling effect?

       ....

    ii)   This drug had a rather unfortunate side effect — what was it?

       ....

d)   Why is aspirin used to help prevent heart attacks and strokes?

    ....

e)   Aspirin molecules are not very soluble.

    i)   How is soluble aspirin produced?

       ....

    ii)   Give an advantage of **soluble** aspirin.

       ....

Q5   **Chlorine free radicals** act on ozone in the stratosphere.

a)   Write an equation to show the action of a chlorine free radical on ozone.

    ....

b)   One chlorine free radical can break up a large number of ozone molecules. Why is this?

    ....

c)   Name two health risks that are increased by damage to the ozone layer.

    1. ....

    2. ....

d)   Since the 1990s, butane has been used as a propellant in aerosols in Europe.

    i)   Explain why alkanes are a better alternative to CFCs.

       ....

    ii)   Suggest why some countries of the world still use CFCs in aerosols.

       ....

Module C6 — Chemistry Out There

Mixed Questions — Module C6

Q6   Ethanol can be produced by **fermentation** or by the **hydration** of **ethene**.

a)   Write a balanced symbol equation for the fermentation method.

....

b)   Describe an advantage that the hydration of ethene has over fermentation.

....

c)   At the moment, this method is a cheap process. Explain why it will soon become more expensive.

....

....

Q7   Hyde tested samples of water from three different **rivers** using the following method.

- 8 cm³ of river water was placed in a test tube.
- 1 cm³ of soap solution was added and the tube was shaken.
- More soap was added until a <u>lasting lather</u> was produced.
- The amount of soap solution needed was recorded.
- The experiment was repeated with boiled water from the river.

The results of the experiment are shown in the table.

a)   Which river contained the softest water? ....

b)   Which river contained the hardest water? ....

c)   Why was less soap needed to form a lasting lather after the water from river A was boiled?

RIVER	AMOUNT OF SOAP NEEDED (cm³)	
	PLAIN WATER	BOILED WATER
A	7	5
B	2	2
C	4	4

....

....

Q8   Paul has two samples of **vegetable oil**, one of which is saturated.

a)   Describe a chemical test that Paul could use to tell which oil is saturated.

....

....

b)   Which of the oils is likely to be better for your **health** if used in cooking? Explain your answer.

....

....

c)   Name a **fuel** that is processed from vegetable oils. ....

CRW41